"Annie hasn't only been my friend for twenty-two years, she's been a mirror the Lord has used to help me see myself more clearly. Reading *Looking for Lovely* is like you're joining us for Mexican— you'll laugh til you snort (or at least we will), cry the good kind of tears, and walk away more encouraged with truth from a genuine friend. That's my Annie." —Molly

"As my oldest friend, kid sister, college roommate, and an honorary aunt to my children, Annie has been a constant in my life for more than twenty-five years. I've seen the stories she tells in real time and can wholeheartedly confirm that she is the friend and woman you think she would be. I'm blessed to be a part of her world and honored to watch God use her mightily." —Haley

"Annie is the friend that cheers up a gloomy day, makes the quiet places not so quiet, and brings joy to the mundane. She shares her life and her stories in an authentic and vibrant way, always leaving me wanting more." —Annie (a different one)

"If you sat down for a coffee with my friend Annie (or her fave, chai tea), you'll probably laugh and you might cry, but you will definitely walk away with a warm heart, encouraged to experience the fullness of life. The same thing will happen when you read *Looking for Lovely*. So grab this book and a good cup of coffee, and let her words be the voice of a dear friend." —Ross

"Annie has this incredible talent of immediately making you feel like you are a part of her inner circle. Her people. Living a few states away from Annie, each chapter of this book feels like we just finished coffee at a favorite local coffee shop. After reading and turning the pages of this book, I know you'll feel the same way. Be prepared to make a new friend. A friend who challenges you, inspires you, and a friend who will forever be in your corner rooting for you!" —Matthew

"When you read this book, you will share one of my life's richest treasures—you will know Annie's heart. On each page, her authentic faith, humor, and vulnerability will challenge and encourage your heart just as it does mine. As her words pierce through fears and fuel your passions, you will undoubtedly have found lovely in this fiercely loyal friend. Trust me on this one." —Misti

"Annie has taught me how to live well, love well, and be well (and eat well). Most importantly, though, she's taught me how to be a friend. Annie is special, and you'll be so much better for getting to know her through her words, I certainly am." —Connor

"Annie is the most beautiful storyteller I have ever met, but I also get to call her my best friend. That means getting her thoughtful advice, having her ask the hard questions, while being the best cheerleader around, and (loud) laughing until it hurts most days. This book contains her raw, heartfelt stories, questions to make you look internally and Scripture to remind you God is walking with you on this journey everyday. I am thankful readers get to experience the joy and love of having Annie as a best friend through the pages of this book. She will constantly remind you that though life is not always easy, there is beauty in the journey if you look for the lovely." —Nichole

ANNIE F. DOWNS

Author of *Let's All Be Brave*

LOOKING FOR LOVELY

COLLECTING THE MOMENTS THAT MATTER

PUBLISHING GROUP

NASHVILLE, TENNESSEE

978-1-4336-8925-3

Published by B&H Publishing Group
Nashville, Tennessee

Author represented by Alive Literary Agency,
7680 Goddard Street, Suite 200, Colorado Springs,
Colorado, 80920, www.aliveliterary.com.

Dewey Decimal Classification: 248.843
Subject Heading: WOMEN \ CHRISTIAN LIFE \
SELF-ESTEEM

6 7 8 9 10 11 12 • 25 24 23 22 21

To the God I met at Radnor Lake,
the One who found me when
I didn't know I was lost,
the One who makes all things new.

CONTENTS

SECTION 3: WHEN I FOUND LOVELY

FOREWORD

A note from Annie

Dear friend,

I am changed. I am different. I have never been the Annie I am today, and that's because God has done something new and miraculous in my life.

I just had to tell you that up front. This is a book about the greatest transformation my life has ever known, and it came on the heels of the most massive breakdown of my life. (Both of these statements made, clearly, with the understanding that there will be greater transformations, and most likely greater breakdowns, to come.)

Transformation and suffering came in a pair. I didn't know they would. But the suffering walked me into something I did not know before. And that's what we're going to talk about here.

I have prayed my guts out for you. That you would feel the Holy Spirit stirring in you as you read, not because of me but because of Him. That His voice would be the loudest in your ears and heart and that this little book, a gift from Him to you, would change everything.

When I write books, I always feel like they already exist. It's not my job to create something new; it's my job to find the piece of art God has intended to be shared and put it down on paper. So I call it a gift without hesitation, not because it is a gift from me but because it was a gift to me as well. I hope I found it as God intended it to be found.

Just a note: some names have been changed, some tiny details shifted, to protect those I have loved, do love, and could maybe love in the future. (You never know. ☺)

Thanks for walking this with me. In some way I feel you here with me as I write, and I hope you feel that I'm there with you as you read, just your friend, across the table at a coffee shop, swapping stories and sharing hope. I want to be there with you. It's for you, after all, all this digging and finding and creating. God has something for you here. I can't wait to see what it is.

Sincerely,

By entering through faith into what God has always
wanted to do for us—set us right with him,
make us fit for him—we have it all together with God
because of our Master Jesus. And that's not all:
We throw open our doors to God and discover
at the same moment that he has already
thrown open his door to us. We find ourselves
standing where we always hoped we might stand—
out in the wide open spaces of God's grace and glory,
standing tall and shouting our praise.

There's more to come: We continue to shout our
praise even when we're hemmed in with troubles,
because we know how troubles can develop passionate
patience in us, and how that patience in turn
forges the tempered steel of virtue,
keeping us alert for whatever God will do next.
In alert expectancy such as this, we're never left feeling
shortchanged. Quite the contrary—
we can't round up enough containers
to hold everything God generously pours
into our lives through the Holy Spirit!

—ROMANS 5:1-5 MSG

INTRODUCTION

Have you ever seen a thunderstorm from the window seat of an airplane? I was flying from Atlanta to Dallas recently, and there, in 17F, I saw the storm to our right, just out my window. The dark, brooding, billowing clouds danced along beside us, the darkest of grays, the strangest of purples—the kinds of colors reserved for only the most wicked of storms. And as we flew parallel with it, I saw sheets of rain drenching the innocent souls below. (Bless them, as we say in the South.) The farm landscape looked like patchwork—one area soaked by the storm, then a dry tract of land and city between, then another region dark and wet. Lightning bolts snaked down out of the sky, and I seriously thought about telling the pilot what I had just seen because clearly THAT IS WHY YOU HAVE ME HERE IN 17F, AIRLINE PILOT, TO KEEP AN EYE ON THE WEATHER.

It was like watching a play, where all the characters were interacting, and I just got to enjoy the show from ten thousand feet above.

From my view? It was awesome, actually. But little is beautiful about sitting under a drenching rain, especially if you have plans for your day or if you lack a roof over your head. But to be next to it? To watch nature move at it's ever-changing clip and have a fuller understanding of the landscape and what weather does to it? It was beautiful.

I'm not as good at seeing beauty in the rainstorms of my life as I am from seat 17F.

I typically sit smack underneath them, watching as my clothes are getting soaked and my straightened hair is getting ruined and what I thought was going to happen with my day (my life?) is getting thwarted. And I find no beauty in that. It frustrates me, it angers me, it annoys me. I look skyward and wonder what I have done to deserve this lot in life. And when I see ugly on the outside—whether it is my body or my circumstances or the hurt in the world, the processing in my heart isn't much better—and the storm from out there usually ends up inside me.

And it is ugly.

I've been struggling with this my whole life: Looking for the beautiful amid the rain, confusion, hurt, and ugly.

My story is like many other women I know—the mirror has lied, and the enemy has whispered for years, and now we can't look at ourselves and find anything lovely, whether it is raining or not. I have looked desperately to no avail. And I've given up. Over and over again. My search has often left me teary, angry, and eating something I regret later. (Thank you, 11:00 p.m. trip to the grocery store for M&Ms.)

I need beauty. I need to see the lovely in my every day. I crave it. Maybe because I have felt it missing in me—in my heart—for so long. Whenever something beautiful is in my sight, I want to devour it. I want to breathe it in, hold it, swallow it, keep it.

But what is it? What is *beautiful*?

We know what we are lacking, like a field in a drought, but do we know what beautiful looks like? Is it a rainstorm or a new dress or a plate of shrimp and grits or Monet's lily pads?

Yes. It is all of those things. And more. So much more.

I got a tattoo a few years ago. I think it is only fair that we start there really. Because I don't like keeping secrets from my friends. I long wanted a tattoo, since I was about twenty, I think. I went through a few different iterations of what I wanted, so I never got one because I figured if I kept changing my mind, that was probably a clue I shouldn't put something permanently on my body.

For many days in 2011 and the first half of 2012, I found myself writing *grace* in cursive across my left wrist. My life was moving at an incredible speed with work, travel, writing, speaking, and trying to keep up wasn't going great. I felt alone, I felt worn down, I felt stretched too thin, mostly by my own decision making. Grace was what I was lacking—toward myself and other people and my schedule. And probably, if I'm really honest, I needed to better reflect God's grace by trusting His plan for my life.

(I'm not sure the science of that or if it's okay to admit. I just know I was frustrated and worried, and I looked up a lot with a "what have You gotten me into" look on my face.)

So every morning I would take my black pen and carefully write *grace* across my left wrist so that as I was driving or waiting somewhere, I could look down and remember the word by which I was to behave. When it's right there on your arm, there isn't much opportunity to be anything else.

At the end of the summer of 2012, I decided to go for it. It had been a hard summer. I had just gone to Scotland for two weeks (a place I tend to run to, as we'll discuss later), and a man I was interested in had just made clear we were never going to be a thing. Or, better stated, he said we would always be just friends, and that's not the label I desired. I was surprised and disappointed and angry at myself for hoping.

So grace. I needed it. I really wanted it permanently tattooed on my wrist. But, because I didn't want it to be distracting every day for the rest of my existence, I wanted it to be white. I am as pale a shade of human as people come, and I cannot tan. I'm either white or red. Pale or sunburned. So a black ink tattoo would be seen a mile away, while a white tattoo on me doesn't stand out at all. I imagined it would almost look like a brand. And that is the feel I wanted. I wanted it literally burned into my skin because I wanted to BE grace. I wanted those five letters to be stuck to me. And I wanted it, then in August 2012, to mark some important shifts of season.

I asked my friend Molly to use her perfect cursive penmanship to write it. Molly and I have been friends since high school, really known each other our whole lives, and she had exemplified grace to me and others a lot. So I figured someone who actually lived it should write it, versus me, the graceless one who just wants to be tagged by it, hoping the truth of the word would actually seep into me.

My friend Hillary went with me to get the tattoo because she knew the dude doing the work. It was simple, short, quick, relatively cheap, and PAINFUL. But when he was done, there in white cursive was *grace*, just as I had imagined. I was in love with it immediately. I teared up, mostly out of pain, but also a little out of joy and love for this little marker of a new season and a new calling.

I absolutely loved it. And I still do. Words are my favorite of all the love languages; having one beautifully inscribed on my arm meant a lot to me and spoke to me about God and His heart and how I should treat myself and other people. It's a really beautiful tattoo.

It reminds me less of who I am and more of who I want to be.

I'm a pretty staunch traditionalist when it comes to writing the first chapter first and the last chapter last, so here we are. At the beginning. Both of us, you and I, are starting this journey together. Toward what? I know, that's a great question.

I think we're walking toward freedom. I think we're walking toward hope. I think we're walking toward the person we really want to be.

So, as I tend to do, I must confess that I'm not great at looking for lovely, at persevering when things get hard, or rejoicing in my sufferings. I wish I could write a book from the vantage point of the expert telling you how to live your life, but that's not it. (This is my fifth book, and I've never once gotten to write a book about something I'm good at—just my struggles and weaknesses. That's so annoying. WHEN DO I GET TO WRITE A BOOK ABOUT HOW TO FOLD A FITTED SHEET . . . because I'm seriously an expert.) So I'm walking this with you, right beside you, asking many of the same questions. And I guess I'm hoping this conversation will be easier because we are having it together.

My last couple of years have been deeply intense and full of learning and walking and experiencing this need to endure, but

I certainly haven't mastered perseverance. I'm just naturally a quitter, not a finisher.

I've spent a lot of time lately in the first part of Romans 5.

Not only so, but we also rejoice in our sufferings, because we know that suffering produces perseverance; perseverance, character; and character, hope. And hope does not disappoint us, because God has poured out His love into our hearts by the Holy Spirit, whom He has given us. (Rom. 5:3–5 NIV)

Before these last few years, I thought HOPE was like GRACE. I thought *hope* was a word we hung up in our houses and tattooed on our wrists and willed ourselves to have. I used to think hope was a gift from God in it's singular form—like love, peace, patience, any of the fruits of the Spirit. But hope isn't a fruit of having a Spirit-filled life. Look at the list in Galatians 5:22–23. No hope mentioned there. What Paul says in Romans, and what you and I know from our lives, is hope is an expensive commodity, not easily won, always fought for, and the result of a process that may take some time.

(That WILL take some time.)

I want you to finish what you start. I want you to be the kind of woman that is absolutely full of hope to where it overflows and splashes on your people. But that comes at a cost. And I hate to tell you this so early in the book because I don't want you to quit reading, but if you want to be full of hope, you have to suffer a bit. You have to find purpose in the suffering so you don't give up. You have to persevere. And when you persevere, your character, your proven faith and tried integrity, grows. And then hope. Hope arrives.

It's that perseverance part though, isn't it? It is for me. I can figure out how to look at a hard moment in my life and muster up the will to rejoice in it. I can feel when my character is being tried and tested and growing. But perseverance? No bueno.

Ever since people started reading my last book, *Let's All Be Brave*, I get a lot of e-mails with the same theme. "I'M GOING TO DO THE THING, ANNIE," they tell me. "I HAVE A DREAM, AND I AM CHASING AFTER IT, AND I'M GOING TO BE BRAVE EVEN THOUGH I'M SCARED."

(They don't always write in all caps, but it sometimes feels like they are yelling with excitement, so I read the e-mails in all caps.)

But my worry is that six months in, they are going to quit. Something is going to get hard, a door is going to close, a whisper of doubt will creep in, a challenge is going to come along. And instead of staying the course, trusting they are on the right path, even if the path doesn't make sense, they will quit.

Abandoned dreams are a heartbreaker to see. Unfinished journeys, where the real joy is just over the hill you never climbed. Those are the broken moments folks lay in bed at night, think about, and regret.

I have some of those.

I don't want any more.

And I don't want you to have any more either.

I want you to be branded by perseverance; I want it to be a marker of who you are and what you are known for. I want people to come to you when times get hard and ask you how you always seem to have a right perspective on things.

I want all of that for me too.

I want us to learn to look for the lovely all around us and collect it, hold it close, and see how God drops beautiful things into our lives at just the right time to help us step forward on our own paths.

I'm honored to be here with you. I can't believe I'm the one God trusted with this work, the work of learning to love the life you have, pressing into the hard on behalf of the hope, and writing about it. But I believe we were meant for this journey.

IN THE ABSENCE OF LOVELY

QUITTER

A few weeks ago two of my best friends from Edinburgh, Scotland, Harry and Esther, came to visit me in Nashville. It was the stuff dreams are made of. I had approximately fifty-two hours to show them my life and my people and my town. And whether I liked it or not, I had to factor in a few hours for sleep. So drop that fifty-two down to about forty. I wanted them to see many places: the deliciously historic Loveless Café, Portland Brew in 12th South (my coffee shop of choice), Radnor Lake, Bluebird Café, Country Music Hall of Fame, Cross Point Church . . . the list went on and on. And with only two lunches and two dinners to work with, how would we EVER get to all the restaurants I was dying to show them?

So I narrowed it down. My best couple friends Annie and Dave offered to host a dinner in their home so Harry and Esther could meet my nearest and dearest Nashville friends. One dinner gone. I insisted one meal be barbeque because, hello, it's the South. And obviously we went to Martin's on Belmont because it smells

13

like barbeque from 1990 in there, and it is so nostalgic and purely delicious. I wanted their clothes to absolutely reek of hickory smoke. For our second evening's dinner, we looked over the menus of two of the best restaurants in town, and they picked Husk, a farm-to-table restaurant that specializes in Southern cuisine.

It was going to be a perfect night. Late dinner at Husk, then we'd walk from there to Broadway because Harry really wanted to see the honky-tonks. (Who can blame him? It's a fascinating sight . . . more the other patrons than the buildings themselves, but thank you, tourists, for being a great sideshow.) Both sides of Broadway are lined with neon-signed honky-tonk bars, each with their own talented live band. Robert's Western World will give you that old-school country music you imagine seeps out of every crevice of Nashville. The Stage offers a rowdier experience, with the band playing the top country songs currently popular on the radio. And then, across the street, there is the bar that is three floors high, each featuring it's own full band.

Locals rarely frequent downtown, but when friends come to visit or a birthday party needs a next stop (a last stop?), we have been known to two-step at Robert's. So when my Nashville friends got wind of us going to the honky-tonks with two Scottish newbies, everybody was in.

Until it started to rain.

As Harry and Esther and I devoured an amazing feast at Husk, my iPhone began to buzz with text messages. One after another, each of my dozen or so friends who were planning to meet us out decided to stay in. Harry was befuddled.

"Because of the rain?" he asked.

"Yeah," I said apologetically, "I mean, maybe we postpone and go downtown tomorrow night? Let me check the weather." And I began fumbling through my phone looking for the weather app.

"No. We're going tonight! Why let a little rain stop us?" Harry insisted.

To be fair to my friends who bailed, it *was* a deluge of rain. But to Harry? It was just a speed bump. He wasn't about to let some water keep us from having fun.

Harry wouldn't let a little rain ruin our night because he always deals with a little rain. Scottish people handle rain better than most because it is a daily occurrence. It may only be for thirty minutes, or it could be an afternoon full of showers, but the people who live there know it's coming and are always prepared with an umbrella or a raincoat. Nothing ugly about it.

Before we even finished eating our dinner at Husk, the rain had subsided, and though the air was thick with humidity as only a Southern summer night can be, we walked downtown and popped in and out of honky-tonks until 2:00 a.m.

It was beautiful.

Harry is not a quitter. It's one of my favorite things about him. He doesn't let rain stop him or midnight slow him down (though I was losing steam); he goes forward with his plan. Weather doesn't interrupt his life.

That attitude reflects in his personal life, his business life, and his honky-tonk life (apparently).

Me, on the other hand? I'm a quitter.

I feel embarrassed writing all of this, but I just have to tell you the truth. I've never been one for finishing strong or finishing at all.

I grew up with a lot of shame. I was about to write that some of it was my fault and some wasn't, but the truth is that it is never a child's fault when they are smothered in shame. It was suffocating. Satan started early with me, whispering into my ear that things were my fault, that I should be so embarrassed when I made a mistake, and that I wasn't good enough or strong enough to be who everyone else thought I could be. So when I think back on the times I quit, what I feel most is how heavy the shame was when I would quit.

I've been trying to think of the first time I quit something because it was too hard. One comes to my mind quickly, probably because it lives close to the surface of my heart and replays in my psyche more than it should.

I started playing soccer when I was in the sixth grade. I went to watch my friend Kristen's game for the first time and immediately wanted to be on the team. It was a game that looked fun and even as an eleven-year-old, I knew my legs were strong and I could kick hard. As soon as Kristen's parents dropped me back off at home, I ran in the house and told my parents I wanted to play soccer. PLEASE AND NOW AND PUT ME ON A TEAM. So the next season I started playing for the YMCA, a little recreational league that ended up being my soccer home for all of middle school and high school.

I played stopper and sweeper. For you nonsoccer people, that means I stood back with the goalie and attempted to keep the other team from scoring. I'm not a fast runner, but I'm a strong player. My motto was, "I probably won't catch you in a foot race, but if you get near me, you're going to lose the ball."

Can you believe I had a soccer motto in middle school? Sheesh. I have a competitive streak a mile wide that is only rivaled by my justice streak. So, you can imagine I'm a different kind of Annie on the soccer field.

I loved playing soccer. I was built for team. It's how I work best. A few of us going after the same goal. (Literally, in soccer.) And as I headed off to high school, with a handful of spring and fall seasons under my cleats, I was ready to play in the big leagues.

As a freshman at Sprayberry High School, I was thrilled to learn my rec league coach was also the head girls' soccer varsity coach. I thought that since he started me consistently during our weekend games at the East Cobb YMCA, I would easily make varsity. So I went into the season with lots of excitement.

The first few weeks of practices are called "conditioning." I almost shudder even just typing that word. It's all about building your endurance and strength, two things I didn't have a lot of and didn't have a lot of desire for. And you don't even get to touch a ball. It's just running and strength training. Every day, a lot of running. A LOT OF RUNNING. And I'm not a great runner.

It's not that my legs or lungs couldn't handle it; it's that my mind couldn't handle it. Even as a young teenager, I knew that was my weakness. The muscle that wasn't strong enough for conditioning was the one between my ears.

(Also, at that point in my life, I should mention, I was already overweight and hated my body. I felt huge and slow, even though, looking back at pictures, I was not that much different in size from my teammates, but I felt very different. Tortoise-like.)

One thing about perseverance I'm slowly discovering for myself: your body can do just about anything your mind decides it can do. I think athletes (real ones, not Annie ones) are built this way. I was not.

Toward the end of the first week of conditioning, we began a drill I'll call leap-frog sprints. If you haven't done them before, CONGRATS and DON'T because they are terrible. The entire team lines up and starts to jog at a slowish pace. The last player in line when the whistle blows sprints to the front of the line and is now the leader of the line and the pacesetter. The whistle blows again, the new last player sprints to the front again. And this happens over and over again, and the team runs around the track that encircles our football field.

I started toward the middle of the group. The jogging part was hard for me. I could hear in my mind, "You're never going to make this; this is way too hard." And as my spot crept closer to the back of the line, panic rose in me. *I'll never be able to sprint to the front of this line,* I thought. *I hate this so much.*

(It's been twenty years since this experience, and I'm telling you, I can still feel the whole thing in my guts.)

The whistle blew for me, I pushed it into high gear and broke out of line, headed toward the front. Tears formed at the edges of my eyes as I realized my fastest sprint was not much faster than what the team was already doing. I got to the front (by the grace of God alone) and was now in charge of the pace. I tried to keep it going, but I was running out of steam. Two girls ran up before me, one at a time when the whistle told them to, as the drill continued. When our line of joggers passed the coaches standing at the entrance gate to the field and track, I quit.

I left the line and fake limped toward the coaches. I told them something about my knee hurting and something about how I couldn't keep going, and they said okay and told me to stretch by the fence.

The girls kept running for a few more laps as I watched.

I didn't make varsity that year. I did get to play on the junior varsity team that year and continued to play for the rest of my high school career, including varsity as a junior and senior, and I was awarded best defensive player on our team.

But quitting that day as a freshman marked me.

As I'm thinking back now, that one decision set a course for me, more than I ever realized it would. Because even today, as a thirty-five-year-old who hasn't played competitive soccer in fifteen years, I look back on that moment and wish I would have done it so differently. It feels like a fork in the road that I never get to return to, and I picked the wrong path.

Gosh, I wish I hadn't quit. Who would I be if I had pushed my mind past the place where it said all the things I couldn't do? What would have been different about my soccer career, my high school experience, my life today, if I had persevered? How would I have seen myself differently in the mirror that night?

I will never know. Which makes me angry and sad, even today.

And I kept quitting. From letting an attacking goal scorer buzz past me on the soccer field, to quitting friendships, relationships, diets, exercise plans, commitments to reading the Bible or praying. You name it, I quit it.

How many times have I promised to have a "quiet time" every day for an entire month only to make it three or four days?

How many times have I signed up for Weight Watchers only to participate for a few months and then never show up again when the weight didn't fall off my body?

How many relationships did I run from because of tension or awkwardness or pain? Instead of being brave and facing the hard moments, I run.

I've never been good at looking past my current pain or suffering and trusting that it will pay off in the future. I think the road has always seemed too long. So when a situation feels painful or scary or hard, I want out.

Today I feel confusion about a man in my life named John. He's single. I'm single. We like being together, but I don't know what he is thinking or where he is going or where we are going or WHAT IS GOING ON. I seem to pendulum swing between THIS MAN IS AMAZING and THIS MAN HURTS MY FEELINGS. And every time I swing toward hurt feelings, I want to let go of the pendulum and fly off into the sunset, like a kid leaving the swing at its highest point. I want to go to Scotland or Atlanta or New York City. Anywhere he isn't.

But it's not him. It's the tension. It's the suffering. It's the hard. I want to run from it. I don't want to sit in it or feel it because my brain tells me nothing is beautiful here. I consider multiple cities my home—Nashville, Tennessee; Marietta, Georgia; and Edinburgh, Scotland. So when things go wrong in Nashville, I find myself searching on delta.com for flights to Edinburgh, hoping to get out of here pronto. Or I call my friends in Marietta to see if they are free for the weekend for me to drive down to visit with them. I find ways to run to other places.

Why? Why do I want to run?

A few years ago, there was Matt. Matt and I had only been on two dates, but I was in a bad place and was scared of him and his feelings. We met about two weeks before *Let's All Be Brave* was due to my editor and proceeded to talk and hang out and go on dates for a month or so. And when I turned in *Let's All Be Brave*, I was an absolute wreck. It had stirred up some painful memories, and the writing pace had been insane, and I honestly just felt like a broken version of myself. Not the humble kind of broken but the literal "something isn't right here" kind of broken.

Matt was awesome. He IS awesome. But pit a new relationship against my broken crazy, and my broken crazy wins every time. We had planned a date for Sunday night because I was headed to the beach on Monday for a few days, and he would be out of town for a week when I returned.

Because it's only a few hours' drive and I wanted my car, I planned to drive to the beach Monday morning. Matt called earlier in the week, and we made tentative plans for Sunday night. Dinner probably, he said, and then maybe a movie. Or a visit to an art exhibit we were both interested in seeing. Sunday night was on, but the plans would be decided later.

And when we hung up, for whatever reason, I freaked out because I didn't know what to do with my feelings. And the broken crazy.

So I jumped on Southwest's website, and I bought a flight to Florida. For Sunday morning. (Just to recap: date planned for Sunday night, so I flew to the beach Sunday morning.)

I spent money I didn't have on a flight and a rental car because I was running away.

When I sat down on the plane, it ended up that a married couple, who are friends of mine, were in the seats next to me. ("It ended up" could be translated to "God planned it.") I teared up as I told them the story. I was running. I was scared. I was quitting something I actually didn't want to quit, just like that soccer drill, because I wasn't strong enough to finish well.

The husband put his arm around me and told me it was okay.

We ordered three glasses of champagne.

And then they told me I needed to see a counselor. I didn't have to fly home, and I didn't even have to fix this relationship with Matt; I just had to fix me.

I've always been pretty hard on myself. I'm not one for physical self-harm but mostly because that wasn't really a thing teen girls did in my day; but the mental self-harm, the self-shaming, and the hateful behavior toward myself has always been a part of my life.

In fact, a little more than a year ago, I wrote in my journal, "Why can't I quit hating myself?" . . . which is almost funny, considering I can quit everything else.

And that question, the question I can't quit about the hate I can't quit is the one I've been trying to answer ever since.

UGLY

I was tiny in the second grade. I remember class-mates making comments about it, someone carrying me up the stairs at Blackwell Elementary School after recess and saying something about how easy it was.

I wore a huge University of Georgia T-shirt with a belt in third grade, like a dress. I had seen a classmate do it, and I thought it looked super cool. It's the first time I recall making a brave fashion-forward choice where I knew I was attempting a style that was just not normal and was not guaranteed to work out right. We stood in line outside the lunchroom, and I tugged at the T-shirt, making sure it was long enough to pose as a dress, and I readjusted the belt to make sure it sat just so.

In the fourth grade, I did a presentation in front of my class with my baby sister, Sally, about how to entertain and care for a toddler. She was two at the time, and I showed my classmates how to read a book to a child and how to feed the child slices of American cheese. Real riveting stuff. My dad videotaped it so we could watch it over and over again.

One day that summer, between fourth and fifth grades, I went downstairs to watch the video. Lying on a beanbag in the cool of our basement playroom, I played the video from just a few months before. The memory of this day is so clear to me that I can still feel my legs stuck against the beanbag because we had the type that somehow always attached to us. My sisters were both in the room—Tatum was just a few years younger than me, and Sally was still a toddler. Some neighborhood friends were over as well. We were all watching together, and I felt pride rise up in me. I had loved that presentation, I loved being the center of attention (shocking no one), and I loved showing my little sister off to my friends in my class, and I was sure it was the finest piece of toddler journalism that ever existed.

"You were a lot smaller then," someone said out of nowhere. "Do you see the difference?"

I hadn't.

But I did now.

Suddenly, in a sentence and in a blink, everything changed for me. There was apparently a size I was supposed to be, and I wasn't it. What I was in fourth grade was okay, but whatever had happened over the summer made my body not okay anymore.

I didn't know what a diet was; at least I don't remember knowing. I was just coming into understanding some things were more beautiful than others, but I didn't put myself on that scale, or any scale for that matter.

I was just Annie.

Until Annie was wrong.

And I finished watching the video with an imaginary blanket of shame draped over me. What I was once proud of, merely minutes before, now I just wished to be over and off the television. I wanted to be alone, to think alone.

At that point the problem wasn't that I thought I was ugly. I didn't put those words around it yet. I just knew there was right, and I was wrong. Whatever I was supposed to be, that video-version of Annie, I wasn't anymore. I was more than, so I was less than.

A year later, as a sixth-grader, I went to my first Weight Watchers meeting with another sixth-grader and her mother. I weighed in at 106 pounds. I don't even remember how long I lasted that first time as a member, but I didn't go to many meetings after that first weigh-in. I quit pretty quickly. But I pretended that I didn't. I wanted people to be proud of me. I figured out praise came when I worked to become the Annie everyone else found beautiful, so I was going for it. I remember lying to my sixth-grade math teacher, telling her I lost four pounds in a day because I wanted her to see I was trying to be the skinny version of me, the fourth-grade Annie, that people liked more. She smiled and nodded, giving me just enough praise to hold my shoulders a bit higher. But it didn't fix me. I didn't lose weight; I gained. And I started to question if things were actually going to get "right" or not.

Those years passed, and they whispered a statement to me I hadn't heard before: I was ugly. I needed to change. My appearance was broken, off, wrong, and I needed to fix it and make it right. Instead of just being Annie, now I had to fix Annie. And fixing Annie was hard, not fun, and I wasn't succeeding.

As my feelings toward myself got morphed and complicated and broken, so did my relationship with food. Food was the enemy . . . and the friend. It was the reason I was here, and I hated French fries for that. But it was also where I went for comfort about my feelings, and I loved ice cream for that. I started dabbling with eating disorders in middle school, but again, because I'm a quitter, I could never really stick it out. I got too hungry to be anorexic, especially during soccer seasons, and I was grossed out by my attempts at bulimia.

So I would just binge. Eat whatever I wanted, whenever I wanted. Whatever it took to feel better, to feel like I could outplay the ugly game, I ate. I would eat too much, and then I would feel guilty and angry and want to punish myself, but I wasn't strong enough or brave enough to actually do it. So I would eat more to not feel the pain.

As a kid, I had just been me; now I was growing to hate me. I was broken and couldn't be fixed; and no matter how hard I tried, I wasn't getting better. I was getting worse. (Thank you, puberty, for seemingly ruining everyone's lives for a few years.)

Ugly chased me. I can see that now. I looked in the mirror with disgust throughout my teen years. I only had a handful of outfits in high school, pretty much wearing the same thing every Monday, then the same thing every Tuesday, and it was like that for the entire week. It didn't matter, I thought. I was ugly, no one was looking at me, so I wore what was comfortable, what covered me, and threw my hair up in a bun. It was a gift for my emotions when my high school decided to require uniforms. Because I was practically doing that myself.

I was sure no one was looking at me anyway. But I knew they were listening.

The only thing I had going for me? My jokes. I had grown accustomed to believing no one thought I was beautiful or found anything lovely about my appearance, but I knew if they took time to get to know me, they would like my personality. If I could get in a conversation, I could usually win people over, even if, as I assumed, they thought I was fat and ugly at first glance.

I had a lot of friends. That part of my soul was still alive and well, the part that loved having as many friends as possible at any one time. (This is still true by the way. Ask anyone who tries to plan my birthday party. The invite list gets ridiculously long because I LOVE MY BIRTHDAY and I LOVE MY FRIENDS and I want ALL THE THINGS TOGETHER.) God made me that way, to love making friends, and that survived somehow, during all the darkness. I often thank God my soul wasn't overtaken by the ugly. While my body and mind suffered, He held my heart, protecting it like the beast prince protects the magical rose in *Beauty and the Beast*. I was committed to my faith, active in the youth group, and truly wanted to be a good Christian.

I loved God. I just hated me.

I had no boyfriends in high school. I went to one dance with a date, but he was my friend's boyfriend from another school, so it absolutely did not count as anything except jewels for his crown in heaven. I had guys who were my friends, even some I thought of as best friends, but none that wanted to date me as far as I knew. (Looking back, I can think of one or two who may have been interested, but my little broken spirit would have never recognized interest from a guy at that point in my life.) There was one boy from a different city that I met on a mission trip, but it fizzled before it even started.

I ping-ponged between fad diets throughout high school. Every major diet you've seen on a commercial, I tried. To no avail. I would lose a little bit, get to a weight, maybe forty to fifty pounds more than I wanted to be, and I would lose steam and quit. And then before I knew it, I would gain back all I had lost and more.

It was a heartbreaking battle I knew was going to be the center of my pain for the rest of my life. What I didn't know, what no one knew, is that my body was suffering from polycystic ovary syndrome, a disease more commonly known as PCOS. My period started weirdly and never normalized to a monthly cycle, and I blamed it on myself—that the way I treated my body was messing up my reproductive system. But the truth all along was that PCOS was causing my body to hold on to weight, have irregular cycles, and just misbehave in general.

So my body and my mind fought on different teams for my entire teenage life. My body trying to tell me a disease was keeping me from the healthiest life; my mind trying to tell my body to get it together or else.

And somewhere, in the corner of me, my soul sat quietly, watching the battle, wondering when rescue would come.

In college I started to turn toward the whispered lies and look them in the face, giving my soul a voice to stand up for the truth. Beginning that day on the beanbag as a nine-year-old, I just swallowed every thought that came into my head. I didn't question anything; I just believed it. If I heard I was ugly, I was. If I heard I was a failure, a quitter, letdown, or unlovable, it was probably true. I spent a lot of time in college wrestling through counseling appointments and discipleship meetings with my mentor, working hard to change my mind and believe truth about who God said I was, not what I heard in my head.

My mind began to change, but my body never did. No matter how much I dieted or worked out (always for short stints—my best friend Candace and I called it my "seasons of self-improvement"), I remained overweight. Painfully so. Not knowing about PCOS, I just thought I was a failure.

I won't bore you with the year-to-year recaps, but let me just summarize by saying I continued to fight this battle for another decade after college. The lies came in, sometimes like a tiny stream of water, sometimes like a raging river. I would diet, lose some weight, and then quit, causing the scale to rebound with gusto. I worked hard to say kind things to myself, to speak life and love to myself and my body, but at the root of everything, the hate was still there. Being diagnosed at twenty-two with PCOS felt like a relief, but it didn't change my body like I thought it would.

I was still me. I was still ugly. And no matter how hard I tried, I could not go back to being innocently nine years old and carefree about my form or my food intake. But I think that's what I always wanted. Maybe it wasn't that I wanted to be skinny or beautiful; maybe I just wanted to be free.

COCAINE

I'm an escape artist of sorts. When things feel too painful or seem too hard, I escape. Sometimes it looks like a flight to Florida but only when I'm feeling REALLY QUITE DRAMATIC. (Bless you, Matt, bless you.) Often my escape tactic is way simpler than that. A nap. A book. A bowl of ice cream. A movie. Television.

And it's not all bad. In fact, I'd say escaping isn't always bad. We need rest for our bodies, minds, and souls. So a bowl of almond milk ice cream isn't the problem; it's what is going on in my mind and heart as I devour said almond milk ice cream.

I love watching television, not just because it takes my mind somewhere else but mainly just because I actually really enjoy watching it. I've got my shows I watch with the girls on a weekly basis. I've got the old series like *Gilmore Girls* and *The Waltons* that I cannot quit, and give me a Food Network cooking competition, and I'll give you my hour. I've got my guilty pleasures, too, most of which reside on the Hallmark Channel.

(Yes, Hallmark Channel, I cannot quit you. Your hyper-emotional love stories set in the Wild West or the constant drama in a small picturesque town off the coast of Seattle are like a flame, and I am a moth. It's your shows. It's your movies. All of it. I'm smitten, and I don't care who knows it.)

Like most of us, I went through my MTV-binging days in college. I cried at the end of *ER* in 2009. I stopped everything to watch *Trading Spaces*. Jimmy Fallon is my best friend even if he doesn't know it, and I'm obsessed with all things ABC drama right now. I love reality television in some of its forms, namely dating shows, and I watch just about any sport you'll put on my screen. Soccer and football are my top two, but if I need a nap, golf is the sport of choice.

A few years ago I got a kick out of watching the reality shows on A&E. *Hoarders* was like nothing I had ever known (except my grandfather's house). I could watch episode after episode of that show and never tire of the ways people absolutely fill their homes to overflowing with what? Brooms, boxes, cats, clothing, old food, DOLLS. Oh y'all, the doll episodes. Nightmares. They will cause nightmares. Houses where you can't see the floor or walls because of stacks of dolls and doll clothes and doll paraphernalia. It gives me the shivers just thinking about it. And I usually would find a way to fill a bag for Goodwill after watching a few episodes. My brain said, "WATCH OUT, ANNIE, THAT COULD BE YOU."

Another show from A&E I love is *Intervention*. It's such a beautiful, full-circle kind of show. You meet the addict, meet his or her family, look at pictures from the addict's childhood, then watch as the addict is followed by cameras, indulges the addiction, and falls deeper into it. Somehow, every episode, the addict doesn't realize an intervention with family and a therapist is about to happen. Drug users and alcoholics are featured mostly. The beauty of the show isn't the demise of the people (clearly) but in the redemption that comes at the end. The show often provides a one- to two-minute update as the hour is closing. The addict has clearer eyes, usually has gained a bit of healthy weight, and has clean hair. The addict hugs a family member and talks about how hard, but good, their time in rehab was.

When Laura and I lived together on 18th Avenue, near Hillsboro Village, we watched a lot of *Intervention*. We would DVR it, recording piles of episodes, and then when we wanted to binge, she would microwave vegetables, and I would pop popcorn, and we'd settle in for a few hours of addiction and redemption.

Laura and I could both relate to the people in the stories, each in our own way, though neither of us has ever been addicted to drugs or a raging alcoholic. But between episodes we would discuss what we thought; we connected it to our lives, and in some instances a character would remind us of people we knew.

I remember one particular episode about a bald man in his mid-forties. He was addicted to cocaine. He did something I had never seen on a previous episode. Sitting in front of a white background, looking straight into the camera, he began to talk about his feelings toward cocaine. He was a little off center from the camera, but his blue eyes bore into the lens and were almost impossible to look away from. He was brutally honest about the drug. He talked about cocaine like a friend he didn't want to have but didn't know life without. He said he wished he could live without it, that he never saw the addiction coming. As soon as he finished a line of coke, he said, he hated himself for it and yet wanted another. He went on and on, and my mouth began to open slowly, in slow shock.

There with my popcorn bowl and Laura right beside me, I began to cry. Not by choice but in a way that was my soul reacting, not my body. Tears flowed down my face faster than I could wipe them away, so I just quit trying. He had just said all the things I didn't know how to say, but I knew exactly what he meant.

Every word.

I felt it deep in my soul, in my high school memories, in my college struggles, in my dinner decisions the night before.

For him it was cocaine. For me it was food.

He defined my addiction.

Every feeling he had toward the drug he hated, I had toward items in the grocery store. It was what I thought was the source of my problems for decades, and yet I could not survive without it. When he looked at me through the television screen and spoke about cocaine, I felt like he was actually saying my own emotions to me.

I freaked out. The tears wouldn't stop. Laura looked like a deer in headlights.

"I'm so sorry," I said, "I don't know what's going on."

But I did.

I had an addiction. For over twenty years I had taken all the pain and hurt and pushed it straight down my throat. For as much as I read the Bible, sat in Sunday school, and made the church my second home, I wish I'd understood, "His ears are open for their cries for help" (Ps. 34:15). Instead of feeling any of the suffering, instead of pressing through the pain and taking it to God, trusting that He heard me, I escaped to anywhere that would feed me, and I stuffed my emotions down by covering them in layers of food.

What if I had found cocaine instead of candy? What if I had drunk beer instead of milkshakes?

I think about it a lot.

I have the same propensity as any other addict; it's just my drug of choice is food.

There's one nutritional counselor in Nashville that everyone knows. Well, once you start saying out loud you have a problem and need help, all fingers point in one direction: Trisha. I had friends seeing her for eating disorders, which I was sure I didn't have because I had quit them every time I tried, and friends seeing her for nutritional support after having a baby or some type of injury or surgery.

I called her. "Um," I stumbled into her voicemail box, "my name is Annie, and I think of food like drug addicts think of cocaine. Call me back when you can."

And she did. I cried through our entire first appointment. I never got on a scale, she didn't tell me what to eat or what not to eat. She just looked at me compassionately yet sternly and said I had disordered eating, whether I wanted that label or not, and that this was a real thing. We talked about hurt and pain and memories and food, and then my hour was up and I left.

Trisha felt like a gift from God. Like He saw my suffering, saw my little soul sitting in the corner looking for rescue, and sent a curly-headed counselor to save the day. Or the Annie, as the case may be.

The view outside her office window was really beautiful. The couch for clients faced that window. Looking across the Green Hills area of Nashville, I often would watch the clouds move or rain pour or the sun set during my appointment. Trisha sat right in front of the window, so as I looked at her and listened or looked her way to speak, I also got to see the beautiful outside.

As we continued to meet, she did begin to instruct me on particular foods to stay away from, for my body and for PCOS and for my soul, and some to increase. (Vegetables.

Always vegetables. Gross.) As much as I liked her, often as my appointment got closer, I would consider canceling. If I hadn't done what she asked, or if I just plain didn't want to talk about FOOD, I would scroll to her name in my phone and prepare a quitter's text.

But I always thought about that view out the window. *Show up Annie,* I would think, *so you can see what's out the window today.* A couple of times that view saved me, as our conversation would pull me from a pit of my own addiction. I would watch the traffic ebb and flow like water. I'd see the sun set behind Green Hills Mall, turning the sky one hundred shades of evening, or watch as the humans crossed from here to there across sidewalks and parking decks. It was the tiny bit of lovely that helped me hang on and show up. God was doing a big work. I knew it, I just had to keep showing up, even when it hurt or felt hard or wasn't AT ALL what I wanted to do.

The view out that window seemed to me the only thing beautiful in the whole situation, and it was the view that kept me from quitting.

LOOKING FOR LOVELY

I've been asking God for a miracle.

I read a book recently that spoke of miracles, of the things God can do that we cannot do, and I realized that in the whole of my faith walk, I haven't often asked God to do the miraculous. I've asked Him to do a lot but not many things that are outside the normal—nothing crazy. Nothing like a blind person seeing or a deaf person hearing.

So I've decided to ask God for a miracle in my love life. That something would happen that would be so outside of the bounds of what humans could accomplish it would clearly be God.

The Bible says to ask, seek, and knock.

Keep asking, and it will be given to you. Keep searching, and you will find. Keep knocking, and the door will be opened to you. For everyone who asks receives, and the one who searches finds, and to the one who knocks, the door will be opened. (Matt. 7:7–8)

So I have been, and I'm going to keep doing it. Asking. Seeking. Knocking. And I'm expecting, fully expecting, to see God do something amazing.

I like looking for things—looking for deals on a new pair of boots, looking for my friends in the crowd at church, looking for the ball to hit the back of the net when a soccer player takes a penalty kick. But I'm not *looking* for a miracle. I'm *watching* for one. It's a subtle difference, but when you really think about it, the way you use the words, and the way I use the words, show you how they aren't exactly interchangeable.

When I am watching, like a sunset or a movie, I know it is going to happen. Things we watch for are bound to happen. We aren't hoping; we're expecting. When you show up at a theater to watch a movie, you aren't there with your fingers crossed, hoping the screen starts showing a film. You expect it. You may have to wait a few minutes for it to start, but it is coming. So you get your popcorn, your SnoCaps, your Coke ICEE, and you take your seat, facing the screen, and you wait, without worry or concern, without question, because you are here to watch a movie.

That's why I'm watching for a miracle. Because I'm believing it is coming. I'm not looking for a miracle like you look for a rainbow, fingers crossed, just hoping you'll maybe see one. I'm watching for a miracle like I watch a movie because I'm expecting one.

I got to Florida on that Sunday morning, flying with my friends, running from the boy named Matt. But don't worry, I had packed all my broken crazy. As I drove the rental car to the above-garage apartment in WaterSound where I would be staying, I thought about Dave and Kelli telling me I needed counseling. I could feel things were off—clearly—but I just thought I might be tired and needing a break from my life, more than anything.

Sheesh, I thought, *I already see Trisha, now I need ANOTHER counselor?* I wasn't sure my finances or my calendar could handle the added strain of an additional appointment. But I trusted them, and so I texted a few friends I knew had spent some time in therapy, asking for a name of someone they recommended.

"Jennifer, I've already told you to see her; here's her number" came back a text from a trusted friend. Sitting upstairs on the window seat of the beautiful garage apartment, with a view of the beach and ocean beckoning me to come lie down and think and read, I dialed her number.

"Hi, my name is Annie Downs. A friend gave me your number. Something is kinda wrong with me. I'm sure it's no big deal, but I think I need to talk to someone about it."

I was looking for healing. I was looking for freedom, relief, change. Something. I needed the broken crazy to go away, and I needed to find the real Annie. The nine-year-old Annie was never coming back, but could I find a healthy adult version of me, with all my past and all my present?

I was looking. I was searching. It was an active move. I wasn't sitting back and watching. Do you feel the difference?

I feel like God has given me a couple of songs to sing with my life. I have to live them first, mind you, but then the choruses seem to just keep repeating. No matter how many stages I stand on or how many conversations I have or how many books I write, a few common themes come out.

1. GOD MADE YOU ON PURPOSE.

We'll talk more about this as we go, but I think it is literally a baseline truth you have to believe. It is a pillar of our faith, especially for women. It may never have been said to you like that before, but trust me when I say it is absolutely true. If you don't believe the way you are is God-made and God-loved, the good and the bad, the tight and the flabby, the old and the new, the strengths and the weaknesses, you are missing out on connecting with God on a level that only comes to those who embrace and love His creations. (And that includes you.)

You're different. Whether you call yourself that or you tend to believe you can just fade into the background, you are different. You are unique. You are the only you there is. God did that on purpose. There are people who see you and see your life and because of the ways you remind them of God, they see Him too. But they see Him differently because of you than they do because of me. It doesn't add pressure for us to be perfect (because I am not), but it just reminds me that I'm put together differently from you. And that's okay. And that's good.

The things you want, the things you love, the things that make you cry, and the things that make you laugh, and the things that make you more angry than you thought you could be—it's a rare combination. In fact, it's a one-of-a-kind combination. Because God made you that way. On purpose.

Your looks. Your loves. Your losses. They are you.

2. GOD MADE YOU TO BE BRAVE.

We were never meant for a wimpy life. Now don't hear me saying we weren't meant for a simple life or a stay-at-home life or a famous life. There isn't a right answer for what a brave life looks like. Just as God made you uniquely, your call to courage is unique as well. But believe me, it is a call. You are called to be brave. You are called to face whatever dragons come into your life and scale the mountains that show up in your view. It may be a literal mountain, a mountain of work, or a mountain of laundry, but it is your journey to walk. And you must walk it bravely. (I wrote a book about it, by the way, if you want to go deeper into what it means to be brave.[1])

But I think we were made for it. Every act of obedience is an act of courage. Every hard yes, every difficult no, every moment of moving and shaking takes bravery. I've felt it in my life, way down deep in my bones, and I've seen it in a hundred lives around me.

To me these two things go hand in hand. One needs the other. You have to be brave to believe you are made on purpose—to go after your passions and walk in who you were made to be. When you believe God made you on purpose, you are willing to be brave because the root questions are already answered.

Am I enough? Yes, God made you on purpose.

Am I alone? No, God never leaves you. The Bible says He loves everything He makes, and He loves you unconditionally, so you are never alone.

If I mess up, if I fail, if things don't go well, am I done? No, you are always loved, you are never alone, you are enough. So be brave, try the thing, trust that if you are pursuing God and going after a brave life, He can fix and sweep up and help you.[2]

I've tried to make these truths real to me. They are not simple, but the level of difficulty comes in waves. Driving down to Brentwood and sitting in Jennifer's office for the first time made me face these statements and ask myself how much I believed them. I was saying these things to audiences, talking about them with my friends, and writing them in books, but was I living them? If I'm supposed to be like this, if this is who I really am, why did I still hate me sometimes? If God made me on purpose, what's with all the broken crazy?

And was I really willing to be brave and tell this woman counselor all the things that trouble me? Like, ALL of them? The stuff strangers knew from Twitter, the stuff friends knew from real-life conversations, the stuff no one knew but someone needed to?

Maybe that's where healing comes from, I thought. Maybe being brave about my brokenness was going to bring healing. I would look for it and hope that was coming along.

Our first meeting went a little like this:

Her: "Hi Annie. Tell me about yourself."

Me: "Oh, hello, everything is fine. My family is perfect. I am practically perfect. No one has ever hurt me; I haven't hurt other people. I'm sure I don't need to be here about anything except this one little sliver of my life—my broken crazy. It's no one else's fault—just my fault—and if you could fix me so I don't kill this relationship with Matt, I would really appreciate it." Ramble ramble ramble—I'm fine—ramble ramble.

And then I sat there and waited for the prescription, the short list of to-dos that would heal me and make me right again. One and done, I thought. Ten minutes of intros, half an hour of me explaining the broken crazy, twenty minutes of her fixing me, and we'd be good to go, an hour well spent.

I thought I needed to be repaired. But my need was significantly deeper than that, and that's pretty much the first thing she told me. I actually needed to be rebuilt. And rebuilding anything that is over thirty years old takes a lot of time and strength and perseverance. All the nuts and bolts of my old ways of thinking were rusted in place, and what the broken crazy had done was reveal that the rust was eroding away at my soul, and it was time to tear down the old and build up the new.

I think that's what Paul must have been talking about in his second letter to the Corinthians.

Therefore, if anyone is in Christ, he is a new creation; old things have passed away, and look, new things have come. (2 Cor. 5:17)

Now we look inside, and what we see is that anyone united with the Messiah gets a fresh start, is created new. The old life is gone; a new life burgeons! (2 Cor. 5:17 MSG)

A fresh start. A new creation. Yes and amen. I needed both of those things. But I also needed the strength of heart to hold on until God could complete the work He had begun.

When I was in college, over a decade ago, I went to counseling for a semester. (Are you sensing a theme in my life? SISTER NEEDS PROFESSIONAL HELP AT TIMES.) One day in my appointment, we began to dig into some of my old habits, old ways, and the lies I so fully embraced: God didn't love me as

I was. I was never enough for Him. I would always be a second-class citizen of the kingdom of God because I wasn't pretty enough and sinned too much. To stick with the rusty metaphor, this may have been the first sign that something was out of sorts and needed to be repaired. Had we caught it there, had I held on for God to complete the work, this most recent rebuilding may not have been so severe.

I left one particular appointment in absolute shambles. I don't know why the counselor let my little twenty-year-old self walk out of the office in that emotional state just because the timer dinged, but we had dug deep and then left the wound absolutely gaping. I went home to the two-bedroom apartment I shared with Candace, still crying, and she wasn't home. Just a few doors down lived two of our best guy friends, so I went over there. Tate was sitting on the couch, watching television. I sat down beside him, crossed my legs, leaned onto his shoulder, and cried for an hour.

"You okay?" I remember him asking. "Do you need to talk about anything?" I think that was his gentle way of saying, "MMMMM, WHAT IS GOING ON? THIS IS FREAKING ME OUT."

I said I was fine, I just needed to sit there, and he let me.

I never went to another appointment with that counselor. I quit. Right there. I cried the night away, and then I walked away from the journey. I didn't let God finish what He started.

I didn't stay on the operating table. I got up and walked away because all I saw was pain and hurt, no beauty.

I felt some of those same pressures and same desires those first few weeks of counseling with Jennifer. Once the Matt situation started to work itself out a bit, and I felt like we were talking through the fears I had, I was ready to stop . . . you know, right before it actually got personal and in my space.

I had walked away from this place before when I was a junior in college, but now I was more broken and wounded and knew that to dig into it would be, well, more. I decided that if I was really going to survive this, it had to be worth it. It had to have some sort of worthy redemption. It had to be beautiful.

I don't know why, but I decided to stick it out this time, to really try to see if there was a healthier version of me that was just on the other side of the broken crazy. There wasn't a beautiful window view like at Trisha's office, but I could feel something beautiful growing in me. Very small, seed-like, but I saw it there. Jennifer and I discussed, at length, what it was going to take for me to stay in the process, to let it work itself out, to not give up.

It was going to take a lot of looking for lovely. I needed to find a reason to show up and not give up on this critical step in my journey. As I thought back over my own life, the beautiful things, though few and far between, were the knots on the rope that helped me keep climbing. In Trisha's office, it was the view out the window. With Jennifer, and the broken crazy, it was the hope that there was something more beautiful just outside my view.

There is a correlation, I'm finding, between beauty and perseverance. It feels like beauty might be knots in the rope you are climbing, gas stations along the cross-country journey, the water stations strategically set up on a racecourse. Beauty is what makes it possible to keep going. And beauty is in the eye of the beholder, isn't it? It's not just in the things everyone sees, but it is what YOU see, what sticks out to you, the unique moments God gives you to collect up and hold and draw strength from.

Had I seen the beauty in finishing a drill with the soccer team, celebrating the strength of suffering together, I wouldn't have pulled up limp.

Had I seen any beauty in me, maybe I wouldn't have walked such an unhealthy path for so long.

I needed to find beautiful if I was going to hang in there. I need it in my life. I need it in my heart. I need it in the bank of my soul to withdraw to when things feel hard. So I decided to start looking.

I have spent significant time over the last few years looking for lovely, actively pursuing it, trying to find it around every corner, and ever hoping it is just right there because I do love beautiful things. But mostly I just don't want to quit anymore. I pulled out old photo albums of trips and memories, and I opened my eyes wider (if possible—I already have froggy-wide eyes) to the world around me.

So as I watch for my miracle and wait for it, I'm looking around for lovely. I'm filling my mind and eyes and memories with good things, good gifts from God, so that my tank is refueled, so that my parched throat is soothed, before the journey continues.

And I usually start looking around 7:00 a.m.

-Section 2-

IN SEARCH OF LOVELY

SUNRISE

Hallelujah!
You who serve God, praise God!
Just to speak his name is praise!
Just to remember God is a blessing—
now and tomorrow and always.
From east to west, from dawn to dusk,
keep lifting all your praises to God!

—PSALM 113:1–3 MSG

I am a morning person. It's almost embarrassing to admit because it sounds like such a grown-up truth, and I try to avoid saying too many adult-ish things. So take me or leave me, but if you take me, you're taking a person who starts to smile and talk about four seconds after her eyes are open.

Also I don't drink caffeine. I used to, and I used to drag around for the first two hours of my morning until caffeine was pumping through my veins. But it's been about seven years since I quit caffeine, and it changed me into a morning person. The annoying kind.

My mornings start around 7:00 a.m. So I'm no "four o'clock in the morning I'm at the gym if you need me and I've already read my entire Bible and emptied the dishwasher" kind of morning person. I like to wake up with the sun, not before it.

A window in my bedroom faces east. When I'm lying in bed, my feet point to the window so I can see directly out. Every night one of my last ritual behaviors (I have about seventeen we can talk about someday) is to open the plantation blinds of that one window. Because that means the next morning, whenever the sun decides to rise, I will too. I set my alarm a little before 7:00 a.m., or a little after, but I rarely need it. The brightness of the first yellowish-white rays will bore into my eyelids, and no amount of tossing and turning will block the warmth, so I'm up. (Now realistically I may still choose to toss and turn and bask in the warmth, but I'm awake. Which is the goal.)

Don't get me wrong; with the right circumstances in place, I can sleep late with the best of them. Give me a blackout curtain, and I can accidentally rise about the same time I'm supposed to be making lunch. But if that became a habit, I'd miss my favorite time of day.

I've long been a fan of sunrises. Whether seeing one over the wing of a plane or from the crest of a hill out in the country or sitting on the beach, there's something calming and beautiful about the sunrise. It's always going to happen, but it is never the same twice.

That 7:00 a.m. hour has sacredness to it at my house. Kidless, manless, it is quiet and still, and nothing wants to move except the morning sun. I can sit on the brown leather couch and just watch out the window as the sun that woke me continues to rise over the church that sits across the street from my home. The normalness of the view is calming for me, and the sun, doing a version of what it does every day, tells my soul that it will happen again tomorrow, just as it did yesterday.

Sometimes I need a reminder that tomorrow is going to come. That simple. No big flashy thing, just a simple reminder that I will make it through to the sunset and, whatever the night holds, tomorrow morning will come. When my heart is broken or when the night seems long or when the darkness feels consuming, please God promise me tomorrow comes in hues of soothing orange and fiery red and a pink that speaks of kindness. His mercies are new every morning, right? That's what the Bible says in Lamentations 3, and I believe it. I believe it when I read it on the page, but I see it in a sunrise. Today is as brand-new to God as it is to me.

I find distinct beauty in the everyday sunrise, the normalcy of it. When the sun hits a certain point in the sky, I don't even have to look at a clock because I know it's 8:00 a.m. and it's time to get moving. And I thank God for those mornings that feel regular. And I thank Him for the ones that feel like art.

I speak each summer at the Bloom Conference in Hawaii. (I know, my life is full of sacrifice and hardship.) But included in the realm of things that actually are kind of hard, there is a six-hour time difference between Honolulu and Nashville. So my first few nights there, when my friends want to eat dinner at 8:00 p.m., my body thinks it is 2:00 a.m., and I can barely keep my eyes open to order from the menu.

The upside? I am bright-eyed and bushy-tailed at about 4:00 a.m. Long before the sun sees the beach, I've changed out of my pajamas and put on my workout clothes—almost always a gray T-shirt, black capri leggings, and my mint-and-gray Nikes—and I'm quietly sneaking out the back door and making my way to the ocean. The beach is about a five-minute walk, so I head to the path when the sun is just releasing its first shades. I try to get to this one piece of driftwood in time for the show to start. The log has been there for three years now and has probably played host to many sitters throughout the days and the years. But a few mornings a year, I sit there to watch the sun rise, to literally watch our globe spin, to watch the night become day.

It's unfair to attempt to describe the sight to you, but I'm gonna go for it. The sky starts a dark blue; the ocean looks black. The stars have retired, but the expanse is early-morning dark. The sky in front of me changes first, lightening in blues until some pinks appear right along the horizon. The top of the sun, on the back side of the ocean, peeks over the water, and the sliver is so small and so bright it looks like a branding iron just out of the fire. It reflects off the water; and as a few minutes pass, the branding iron doubles in size. The sky responds to the fire colors in a subtle way at first, spreading across my whole view. I work so hard to strike the balance between watching it and taking pictures for Instagram and trying to memorize every second so I can keep it forever. I want to eat it. I want to hold it. I want to freeze it in time, every time. Because it's not just the reds and yellows and sunrise shades; it's the aqua greens of the water and the blues of the sky above my head and the whites of the clouds. I see tones at play that don't have names and can't be described. And the sun slowly shows more and more of its morning redness, and the ocean mirrors it, and the sky mirrors it, and it seems like I can see fifty different colors, and within fifteen minutes my entire view is an explosion. It lasts for three to four minutes, and then the sun is up, the sky is blue, the clouds are white, and the day has begun.

God orchestrates it. I know He does. Something like that doesn't happen without a Conductor. And yet it can't be timed, and it is not a predictable show. It is an incredible artistic gesture by God for lots of people, but it often feels particularly for me.

I love when the darkness ends, don't you? Maybe that's the whole thing. Maybe I find so much breathtaking beauty in the sunrise not so much because of what is starting but more because of what it signals has ended.

LOOK FOR LOVELY

Set your alarm tomorrow to see the sunrise. Don't tell me you don't know when it happens because one Google search will tell you the exact minute. (Oh technology, we love you.) About twenty minutes before the sun is to rise, get in a place where you can see the eastern sky. That way you see how dark it is before dawn. You know it in your heart. If your life feels so dark that sometimes you have no idea where the light is going to come from, go there early and watch the sunrise.

And afterwards? Read Psalm 19. You'll thank me later.

RYMAN
AUDITORIUM

My heart, O God, is steadfast;
I will sing and make
music with all my soul.

—PSALM 108:1

It's called the Mother Church of Country Music. The Ryman Auditorium.

I had to come here to write about it. So that's where I am today, sitting in the balcony, section 15 to be exact, and looking across the room in broad daylight is a unique experience. I've only been here at night, attending concerts and speaking events, so to see the sun shining through the stained glass panels in the back of the balcony at 10:00 a.m. with all the pews shining under the lights, is a different view. And it is interesting as people on guided tours weave in and out of rows and sections, taking pictures of the room. I want to yell: "YOU ARE MISSING IT. YOU ARE MISSING THE HEART OF THE

PLACE," because when you sit here in the dark, at a sold-out show, and watch the face of the performers as they come back on stage for the encore, you see the heart of the Ryman.

I can't come here without thinking about the history of this place. It was built because revival was breaking out in Nashville in the late 1800s, and they needed a place to meet that would hold more people than the revival tents. God showed up and showed out in this city in 1886, and this building exists because He did. Though no church meets here anymore, and not every act on the stage honors Him, you can't deny that this place was built with a purpose; it was meant to be a house for the Lord. You can feel it. So yes, it is the Mother Church. It is a church. It may not always be treated as such, but that's the foundation. There is so much history here—from Elvis to Minnie Pearl to Brad Paisley, and all that history sits in this room. It's absorbed in the walls and wooden floors, and it is palpable.

It's a beautiful old theater. The downstairs has rows and rows of pews made of warm golden wood in a half-moon shape, facing the elevated stage. The upstairs balcony looks much the same, a sea of wooden church pews with a steeper incline. The lighting rigs hang above your head, and the ceiling is old wood slats painted barely mustard yellow. Under the balcony are old light fixtures and painted pipes, and it looks exactly as you would picture a church built around 1900. The stained glass windows, across the back wall of the balcony and the back wall of the downstairs, are in groups of six; four different colored squares are on the bottom, and two churchy-shaped, pointed ones are on top. Red, yellow, green, and blue—each panel is just one full color. There is nothing complicated about the windows; they are just beautiful.

That's the feel at the Ryman. It isn't complicated, but it's beautiful. You are either upstairs or downstairs. You squeeze into your seat on the pew, doing the best you can to sit with your back touching the metal plate with your seat number on it. The stage is big, and it is said that there isn't a bad seat in the house. In my seven years of "research," I have found that to be true. All the artists I have ever seen perform there at some point unplugs and steps away from the microphone. They step toward the front, take their ear pieces out, and just sing. It's something about the acoustics and the way they perfectly created this room for music. When Drew Holcomb sings "Tennessee" a cappella with no microphone, the crowd goes silent, and everyone is in awe . . . until the moment he invites the crowd to sing along. And then, because the room is full of Nashville people, the sound swells in four-part harmony, and I'm not kidding—just writing about it makes me tear up. The sound of this town singing in this room is moving.

It is Nashville. Swirling in this room is the history and the echoes of over a century of concerts and performances and worship services. I feel God here. It's revered by artists, honored by the city, and loved by audience members. The Grand Ole Opry still does shows here a few times a week, and it makes me miss my grandmother Kath because I remember watching the show on her little kitchen television while we ate biscuits with butter.

Maybe it's the pews, or the openness of the balcony, or the way it feels like a really small room, but you never feel alone in the Ryman. Across the street at the Bridgestone Arena, where our hockey team plays, and monster trucks race, and all the massive tours come through, you can feel like you are alone even while you are in your seat at a concert surrounded by thousands of people.

But here at the Ryman, you feel like you are sharing the experience with everyone, like y'all are all in this together. You are not alone.

The tickets aren't cheap usually, so I look at the weekly Ryman events e-mail and plan how to save up my money, and I e-mail friends to schedule about when we all want to go. But it's pretty frequent for me, a few times a year. I'm learning that I need it.

As I'm looking for lovely, as I've spent the last few years really trying to find what makes me feel alive and full of peace and like the best version of me, one of the answers is sitting right in this room. Every time I'm here, I remember another time I was here. They build on top of one another to create this folder full of memories and moments that make me feel at home.

Nashville has a poster company called Hatch Show Print. For each Ryman show they create a unique poster that only people who attend the show can buy. If you want to see a collection of moments that remind me of lovely times, all you have to do is look around my house at the posters from the shows I've attended. Each of them has a really sweet history for me, a memory, a moment I don't want to forget.

Lady Antebellum's print is from April 2010, the first time the megastar country group ever headlined the Ryman. It was a huge night, a really life-changing experience for the band and for us, their friends. I'll never forget how Hillary wrote a personal note to each friend she invited, and she stuck it in the envelope at will-call along with a ticket. Charles Kelley led the crowd in "Amazing Grace," along with Hillary and Dave, and we all cried that night, watching our friends' dreams come true. The poster sits on the mantel in my living room, and I remember the joy of that show every time I look at it. I also remember their hard work, their perseverance, how they have gone after their dream of a life in music and succeeded. It makes me proud.

Ingrid Michaelson's poster hangs on my living room wall, a reminder of the night in 2014 when she cried while playing "Somewhere Over the Rainbow" and the cast of the ABC show *Nashville* sat in the two rows in front of me.

Every Christmas my family comes to town, and we all go to Andrew Peterson's "Behold the Lamb of God" concert. We've sat in as many different sections as years we've seen the show and never once had a seat that wasn't spectacular. That poster is seasonal decor for my house, but it comes out every holiday season.

One of my favorite radio shows, *This American Life*, is hosted by Ira Glass. In 2014 he came to the Ryman to do a night of storytelling. So yes, that Hatch Show Print hangs in the hallway beside my coat closet. Kelley and I went together but couldn't find seats next to each other, so we ended up sitting one row apart and just texting each other every time Ira said something profound. I pass that poster when I head to the laundry room, and it reminds me to ask myself if I'm still going after my own dreams.

In 2012 my all-time favorite band, Mumford & Sons, came to the Ryman for a three-night stand. I went. Twice. I originally purchased tickets for the first night of the Mumford shows—a Tuesday—and the show had some kerfuffles. (Namely, Marcus Mumford ran off the stage to vomit twice.) So when a friend offered me a ticket to the Thursday night show, better seats, less vomit, I was all over it.

If I had to do it again, I would go all three nights, even the first one that was kind of pukey, because it was one of the most beautiful experiences of my life. Every seat was full, everyone was dancing and singing along, and you could just tell, both nights I was there, that the men in the band were in heaven. So was I. It filled some tank in my soul that I didn't know had run dry. I think that's why I couldn't resist Thursday night—I was still thirsty, I was still in need, I wasn't satisfied.

That Hatch Show Print from my two-out-of-three Mumford attendance sits on my mantel next to Lady A's poster. It has a beautiful illustration of the Ryman on it, along with the dates and the band name, so it may be my absolute favorite one so far.

I sat alone once at the Ryman, during a hard part of the broken crazy, the winter of 2014. A weird turn of events led me to that single seat. Some friends had come in town to see the Secret Sisters and Nickel Creek. We had purchased four tickets, and then one more friend decided to come, so she bought a ticket alone. It was two sets of BFFs and me, so it made tons of sense for the four of them to sit in the set of four tickets we had and for me to sit in the seat alone that was just one section away from my friends. Sitting alone didn't stress me out. In fact, I was kind of looking forward to it, knowing how my guts really loved being in this room. And really once a show starts, you don't talk to your people anyway. In fact, I think I was in section 15 of the balcony! (Hilarious that I'm sitting here now as I write.) They were on the edge of section 13, so I could clearly see all of them.

It was good for me in a lot of ways. It was good to have to think and sit in my section. To listen to the music, to hear the bluegrass and the harmonies and the banjos, and just to feel it. For me, there was no processing with my friends between songs, and I did have to battle the lie that whispered in my head that surely people around me think I am a loner and a loser, but finally, I was swept away by the sounds.

The posters remind me of the moments when the Ryman reminded me that live music does something for my heart, not just my ears.

I wanted to remember how the lower level feels today, too, so I've moved down to section 2 on the far right of the floor level, almost opposite to section 15 in the balcony. And still the view of the stage is perfect. Fewer people milling about, so little tears in the corner of my eyes aren't quite as embarrassing.

I just love this room. I love how it reminds me that Nashville is my home, and I love how it stands out, not only in the downtown skyline but in the stories of this town and in the hearts of the patrons. In a town full of concert venues, only the Ryman plays with the idea it might be holy ground. The reverberating of the voices and the instruments on the back walls of this sanctuary that was built with sound quality in mind go straight to the middle of who I am and expand there, filling whatever holes have grown.

LOOK FOR LOVELY

Well clearly, if you are in Nashville or visiting Nashville, I'm going to tell you that you MUST go to a show at the Ryman. (And look around, because I'm probably sitting in the audience with you!) But if you aren't in Nashville, I bet there is a place in your town—a building or venue that speaks to your soul in a way that's unique to you. Maybe it's a theater or a library or a church. Go there, give yourself to it, and see what God does for you in that place.

TRAGEDY

Come to me, all you who are weary and burdened, and I will give you rest. Take my yoke upon you and learn from me, for I am gentle and humble in heart, and you will find rest for your souls. For my yoke is easy and my burden is light.

—MATTHEW 11:28–30 NIV

 When my mom's first text of the day is, "Are you awake?" I always worry. It means she needs to call, and it means something is wrong.

Always.

And today started that way. I was awake. So she called to tell me a lifelong friend had been in a car wreck, and his wife, a friend of mine from college, was killed. It sucked the breath right out of my lungs. Deep sadness interrupted my Friday morning. And as I leaned on my dresser in disbelief, about to dry my hair, another friend sent a text about her family emotionally imploding the night before. Heartbroken, she had locked herself in the basement and didn't want to come out. And yes. She is the mom.

I sat down on the chair in my room, wide-eyed. I could have driven across town to be with her, but since I did not have a key to her basement, that would not be totally helpful. I could do nothing to help her or my friend who had just lost his wife.

My phone buzzed. An update about an emergency appendectomy that happened two days before. GOOD GRAVY. IT WAS NOT EVEN EIGHT O'CLOCK IN THE MORNING YET.

It was too much.

Where is the beauty in any of this? How am I supposed to tell you to look for and find beauty when tractor trailers run amuck and kill people you love? When conversations turn to fights turn to yelling matches turn to silence and separation? When surgeries are sudden and painful and expensive?

Just last week I heard a story of a friend's broken heart over a relationship that didn't work. My mind goes back there. When he explained it, he said, "This is the most profound pain of my life. But it also feels sacred." You know me, I was telling him to ask God to HEAL HIM NOW and LET THE PAIN END, and he's sitting there, shattered, saying, "No. I need this. I need to know God here. It feels important."

Sacred.

I don't think like that in sadness. I'm not thinking like that today. I'm thinking about how I want to lay my head on my desk and cry, how I want Jesus to come back right now and make it all right. This doesn't feel sacred; it feels unfair. In every situation. I want the betrayals to end and the deaths to stop and the pain to leave. I don't want to persevere through this or learn something new or find beautiful.

I just want to be sad.

So I turn to Ecclesiastes 3, looking for some sort of balm to heal my soul, or at least quiet the burn. And the heading of the chapter is "The Mystery of Time."

Yes, mystery.

There is an occasion for everything,
and a time for every activity under heaven:
a time to give birth and a time to die;
a time to plant and a time to uproot;
a time to kill and a time to heal;
a time to tear down and a time to build;
a time to weep and a time to laugh;
a time to mourn and a time to dance;
a time to throw stones and a time to gather stones;
a time to embrace and a time to avoid embracing;
a time to search and a time to count as lost;
a time to keep and a time to throw away;
a time to tear and a time to sew;
a time to be silent and a time to speak;
a time to love and a time to hate;
a time for war and a time for peace.
(Eccl. 3:1–8)

God gives us permission to feel. There's no demand on your life to bite the bullet and be stronger than the hurt and pain. Yet the directive is the same: rejoice in your sufferings, persevere in them, let your character grow, and watch as hope blooms.

But ugh. I don't feel that today. I feel the suffering. I can't see into the future enough to see what hope is going to look like in any of these situations, but I do know that I'm being given the chance to stand at the starting line again, to start back at Romans 5:3 and stay on this path until Romans 5:5 is living and active in me again.

I'm not sure I'll find beautiful in this. But the only way to truly see beauty, for my heart to grow in capacity and in ability to love and cherish, is through pain and heartache.

In the most simple and not profound way, I think about when I got my ears pierced in middle school. It hurt like whoa, but I finally fit in with all my friends and quickly bought a pair of tiny silver dolphins to wear. I also, soon after that, purchased a pair of earrings where the front was a pig's face and the back was the pig's legs, so it looked like each pig on each ear had stuck it's head through my earring hole and it's body still hadn't come through. So that should give you some idea of my fashionista ways of eighth grade.

I had a friend who, early in high school, decided to turn his pierced ears into gauges. You know, when people stretch the hole in their ears from simply holding an earring to holding wooden dowels of different sizes. I've never done it, but I have heard that it hurts like crazy each time you upgrade to the next size gauge. But it's for a purpose. The only way you can fully experience the next level is by experiencing some pain.

Clearly this doesn't compare to the actual tragedy of losing a spouse or family arguments, but I think of it because I remember that there are times in our lives when we choose to experience physical pain in order to increase our joy.

It's what happens in the gym, isn't it? We (pronoun used loosely here, probably should say "you") press through the pain and the hard for the adrenaline high that comes after a serious workout. You are willing to feel the pain for the greater good on the other side.

I look at my own story, at the tragedy that happened in my life, and my heart, at nine years old, when I stopped being Annie and started trying to fix Annie and make her right again. For years after that I worked hard to cover my feelings, to eat enough that it stuffed down the pain, to escape hurt at any cost.

I can see that as a thread throughout my story. I don't want to feel pain or sadness. I want to avoid it.

I have an adult onset allergy to dairy. In my former life as an eat-whatever-you-want type gal, ice cream, yogurt, cheese, and milk were normal staples in my everyday. So those types of foods were central to my stuffing down of feelings and smothering of pain. Just as milk is used to calm the heat of spicy food, I used it just the same—to soothe and coat and cover all that was painful.

And then in 2013, I couldn't do that anymore. When I ate dairy, my face and chest and hairline and head and neck would break out into a rash and begin to itch under my skin. I had to cut it out of my eating habits.

Just like that, instead of eating ice cream until my pain subsided or disappeared, I had to look at my pain. And feel it. I had to sit in the uncomfortable and unfamiliar areas of hurt and figure out what to do with the actual feelings and the experiences. And when the broken crazy got loud that summer, I just couldn't stuff it down.

No more smothering. No more pain avoidance. No more ice cream.

Those first days of walking away from dairy, the first days I really started to take my health seriously and listen to what my body wanted, so much pain bubbled up and bubbled over. So much trauma from my childhood and adolescence began to surface when it was no longer sedated. And I had no choice but to feel it all—the hurt from what others said to me, the pain of carrying secrets, and the worry and anxiety that riddled my mind. I didn't know how to talk about it. Though it had been years since the things happened, I really only started to feel them when I quit drowning my sorrows in milk.

Over the past three years, my experience of pain and hurt has deepened. One of the hard parts of writing books is that not everyone in your life gives you permission to tell the stories you live, so to honor others, there are some stories I cannot tell. But within the last few years, I have experienced depth of heartbreak that I truly did not know was possible. I have never felt more alone, more abandoned, more misunderstood. While I was digging through old pains and problems, the world did not stop, and sin did not let up, and so for six or so months, I was pelted from the inside and the outside with more pain than I had previously known.

And I survived. I didn't quit. I didn't walk away from the pain or give up on life. I walked all the way through it, holding the hands of many trusted friends and my counselor, and here I am on the other side. My counselor was right; my capacity to see beauty has increased in a much bigger measure than the pain I felt. My ability to feel the depths of something good was strengthened by my choice to feel the depths of pain. I don't exactly know how it works. I just know the more I hang on and feel, the more I am able to feel; and each time more balm gets rubbed into the wounds of my soul.

It's sacred, right? Feeling God right here, in the middle, is just as my friend described. Purely sacred.

So looking for lovely is not some sort of cheerleader chant. I'm not waving pom-poms at you or dressing like Pollyanna and trying to convince you that things shouldn't hurt if you are "doing this right." In fact, I'd say it's the other way around. It's not about pretending everything is beautiful and nothing is ugly and you have no questions or doubts and picking out the beautiful in your everyday is going to protect you from anything hurting ever. It's about feeling the pain, letting the sufferings be a part of your life, embracing the Romans 5:3 moments so you can process through the Romans 5:4 days so you live a Romans 5:5 hope-filled life.

If you aren't experiencing pain, you aren't experiencing beauty. Darkness makes us appreciate the beauty of the light. If you aren't allowing yourself to feel the hurt, sadness, loneliness, and disappointment this fallen world has to offer, you probably aren't feeling the fullness of the joy and beauty the redeemed moments have to offer.

There is nothing beautiful about a tragedy. My friend dying in a freak car accident? Not beautiful. And we feel that. Deeply. The pain of broken families and broken hearts sometimes is deeper than words can describe. But there is beauty in choosing to feel that pain, in calling hurt what it is, and not pretending everything is okay.

Whatever tragedy you have experienced or are currently living through, the most beautiful thing you can do is LIVE. Keep walking, keep weeping, keep eating. Don't ignore the hurt. Don't attempt to avoid it and just move on with your life. Feel it all, and invite people in to feel it with you.

LOOK FOR LOVELY

I don't know what you need, friend. But maybe today is the day you pick up your phone and call a person and say how bad it really is. Maybe it's time to call a tragedy a tragedy.

FARMERS' MARKET

But the seed on good soil stands for
those with a noble and good heart,
who hear the word, retain it,
and by persevering produce a crop.

—LUKE 8:15 NIV

A few years ago our little neighborhood decided to start hosting it's own farmers' market. Every Tuesday from May through October, the field beside the picnic pavilion fills ups with local farmers bringing the spoils of their labor.

I've always loved a fresh farmers' market. Maybe it's the romantic in me, and I feel like Kathleen Kelly from *You've Got Mail* when Joe Fox buys a mango as they stroll through the Upper West Side market, or maybe it's because I was the girl who would read lots of novels about the olden days when everyone was a pioneer and working in the fields first thing in the morning. But for me, there is something about shopping at a farmers' market that makes me feel connected to a simpler time.

I grew up going to Burger's Market. It's just down Canton Highway from my parents' house, and the storefront looks the same today as it did when I was a kid. Big red letters spell out BURGER'S MARKET above the doors with a cutout of a red tomato between the two words. Instead of a parking lot in front, there is a nursery full of rows of live plants and flowers. My grandmother used to love to buy hanging plants from Burger's. It was never a quick decision, and I would shuffle and sweat as I stood beside her on the asphalt under the midday sun while she picked between the purple flowers and the light purple flowers.

Inside, in the open-air store, is every type of in-season fruit and vegetable. Mom always sent me to get squash and tomatoes while she got potatoes and onions. In the back are some local Georgia things like peanut brittle and jams. Burger's is wall-to-wall fresh food. And even with all the issues I had with food, I could look around Burger's and think it was awesome. I think that little place deep down in me that longed to be healthy found a little home there in Burger's.

When I got to high school and met a football player with the last name Burger, I thought I had met a celebrity because Burger's Market was such a frequented stop for our family.

My parents still stop in there often, and I do too. Whenever I'm driving back to Nashville from Marietta, Burger's is my last stop as they offer fresh-made boiled peanuts, a delicacy that is a must for your life. Georgia peanuts, still in their hard shell, are boiled in water with a big heap of salt, and they sit there for lots of hours. By the time they are ready to eat, the shells have softened up and are easy to pry open with your teeth and the peanuts inside are salty and soft, the consistency of cooked lima beans. If you don't know them, you need to know them. (I literally cannot find them in Tennessee. It's hard on my emotions.)

So each week here in Nashville at the 12th South Farmers' Market, my soul connects back to being with my grandmother and mom as each tent from each farm is full of only in-season foods. And as they set up, they turn a field of grass into a horseshoe-shaped market, with booths from across Middle Tennessee on either side of the path. I try to go almost every week, even if it is just to get a carton of strawberries or some sherbet from the lady with the rolling ice cream cart and big umbrella. This will not shock you, but my main motivation for attendance is not the vegetables, but neither is it the sherbet. While I am always glad to see what fresh produce makes it to our neighborhood, I'm more excited to see my neighbors.

Nashville is split up into little villages all over town. And many of my friends call 12th South, our little corner of Music City, home. Or they are like me, claiming to be a 12th South resident when I clearly live in Oak Hill. (I claim 12th South because it's where the cool kids live, and I want to be cool. Okay? Okay.) So every Tuesday the likelihood of running into a friend is high because everyone pops down to the farmers' market in the afternoon.

On a normal summer Tuesday, I drive over to Annie and Dave's house, and she and the kids and I will grab our reusable grocery bags and walk down to Sevier Park. We slowly walk the horseshoe-shaped market, her arms loaded up with vegetables, while I pick out a few that I know I like, but definitely feeling the magnetic pull to the goat cheese guy. HE MAKES PIMENTO GOAT CHEESE. I cannot resist him.

Annie and I tool around for an hour or so, even though you can lap the farmers' market in less than ten minutes, because we stop and talk with friends about every ten feet. Miranda is over at the local ranch booth, getting some fresh meat, so I say hi and ask about her new restaurant venture. Amy and Jon are stocking up on blueberries as I overhear her telling Annie a recipe she is dying to try with blueberries in lasagna. Amber, Hillary, and Laura are sitting at a picnic table, talking over popsicles, so I sneak over to interrupt. I see Katherine pushing Henry in his stroller, and I yell a hi to them. Heather's three-year-old daughter Annabelle runs by, and I snatch her up for a hug, and we walk toward the Mennonite farm tent.

Under the cool of the shady pop-up tent, they have three long tables covered in red-checkered tablecloths and shaped like an upside down U. The left side has carton after carton of strawberries. There are some radishes poking out of wicker baskets toward the back corner where two tables meet like an L. They have some honey and a few loaves of homemade bread beside their cash registers. Then the right side is just a mass of vegetables. Lettuces, onions, kale, yellow squash, cucumbers, and snap peas. At the front are a few huge watermelons that are mostly green, with a few light yellow spots.

Annabelle and I walk out of the sun and into the shade of the tent, and she begins to point to different vegetables and say their color. And when she does, I tell her the name of the produce. We go through the three tables over and over again, to the point it is awkward for me not to buy something from them, so I grab some kale and strawberries to use in my breakfast smoothies. One of the watermelons is sliced, so she and I both grab a little slice as we walk out and thank the lovely Mennonites.

I pick out the slimy black seeds from her piece before she attempts to digest them. I pick them out of my slice too, and flick them into the grass, silently apologizing for possibly planting a watermelon vine in the middle of Sevier Park.

We walk back to her mom, Heather, and we chat for a bit. Then as the afternoon turns to kid dinnertime, everyone kind of moseys back to the street where they live (or where they park, as is the case for me).

But I can't get those little seeds out of my mind. The tininess of the seed versus the monster size of that beautiful watermelon we sampled. I see the beauty across the farmers' market in the colors and the textures and the vegetables and how our Earth produces just what we need to be healthy.

But again my mind keeps going back to the watermelon seeds. Something about those slimy little seeds has me tearing up.

Those who sow with tears will reap with songs of joy.
Those who go out weeping, carrying seed to sow,
will return with songs of joy, carrying sheaves with them.
(Ps. 126:5–6 NIV)

There is something beautiful in the small seeds. And I need to be reminded of that. When my heart is broken and I am weeping, when tragedy hits and I feel like the tears will never stop; when I feel like I've cried an ocean, the Bible says they are just seeds. Then the seeds are planted, covered in dirt, and persevere through the season of growth. Again there's that perseverance. There's that reminder to not give up. Because somehow I sow tears and reap joy. And the joy will be greater.

I'm a crier; it's one of my go-to emotions. At the doctor's office this morning, I cried. Driving home from a funeral last week, I cried. When he broke up with me in a text, I cried. (And later rolled my eyes.) I have sown my fair share of tears, and to be honest, I cannot imagine how God can take that sadness and multiply it in size and turn it to songs of joy. I just don't see the math in that.

But I do see how it adds up when I look at a watermelon at the farmers' market.

Just like a watermelon's seeds are dwarfed in size by the watermelon itself, I see that my weeping and my tears will be minimal compared with my joy. I will go out with seeds and return with sheaves. I can pictures sheaves of wheat thanks to Burger's Market and my local farmers' market. I can feel the texture of those tiny seeds in my hands because I picked them out of Annabelle's slice.

I'm looking at some of the joys I'm experiencing in my work—getting to write, having an office with a beautiful desk built by my friend Blake. I've never done this before, but I'm trying to see this as sheaves. This is the multiplication of the tears I sowed when things didn't go well for me professionally—when I got the repeated noes from publishers, when I've had to part ways with people who worked with me, when someone writes a cruel review of my writing on the Internet. Those tears have always seemed so large, but when I really think about it, the Bible is right. These joys are much greater than the sadness.

And what I'm almost too afraid to think about, if I'm being honest with you, is what this means for the tears I've cried over my singleness. Because ... THEY HAVE BEEN CRIED AND WILL BE CRIED AGAIN. How can something dwarf the heartache and loneliness I've felt my whole adult life? How can that be? I question if it can, to be honest. That's just the truth of what I feel. I love my life, and I'm so grateful for all I have, but it certainly isn't the kind of joy that makes the tears seem tiny.

But then, slimy watermelon seeds. I have to cling to the truth of what will become of those slimy watermelon seeds. That in their season, they will each become lots of watermelons (though hopefully not in the middle of the farmers' market grass), just as every tear I've sown will grow into something joyful and beautiful far grander than I ever expected. What God will do with my seeds, when I return with songs of joy, is grow them into something full of color and health and variety and joy and blessings for others—just like the farmers' market.

I'm believing what I cannot see because of what I can see. And that's the kind of moment that matters to me—the kind I hang on to, the kind I call lovely, the kind that sticks to my heart and reminds me over and over again of who our God is and how He works.

LOOK FOR LOVELY

Buy a watermelon, the kind with seeds. And look for yourself.

ATHLETES

You've all been to the stadium and seen the athletes race. Everyone runs; one wins. Run to win. All good athletes train hard. They do it for a gold medal that tarnishes and fades. You're after one that's gold eternally. I don't know about you, but I'm running hard for the finish line. I'm giving it everything I've got. No sloppy living for me! I'm staying alert and in top condition. I'm not going to get caught napping, telling everyone else all about it and then missing out myself.

—1 CORINTHIANS 9:24–27 MSG

I love sports. For as long as I can remember, watching sports and playing sports have been a part of my story and my family life. Because my dad never had any sons, he would always take me and my sisters with him to watch games.

As an adult now, someone who has friends with kids, I'm still superimpressed that when my dad bought two tickets for an Atlanta Falcons game, he would invite me to use one of them, instead of, you know, one of his friends. I mean, I'm pretty fun to hang out with as an adult, but as an eleven-year-old? Not as much.

Dad once took me and my two sisters to an Atlanta Braves game. I was in middle school, so was Tatum, and Sally was just a little kiddo, probably four or five. Dad bought great seats, just a few rows behind first base. It was July, and we all wore our jean shorts and Atlanta Braves T-shirts. (Maybe not Dad. He only wears khaki shorts and button-up shirts.) We grabbed Cokes on our way to the seats. It was a hot day because JULY and ATLANTA. We knew it was hot going into it, but we had no idea how incredibly hot.

One inning. We lasted one inning. My poor dad bought the tickets and Cokes and drove us forty-five minutes to Fulton County Stadium for us to see three men try to hit the ball in the hot July sun. Then, after about half an hour in the stadium, the weeping and gnashing of teeth, the "PLEASE DADDY, I AM MELTING," the tears from little Sally as her face turned beet red and the sweat soaked her hair, we left.

That should have been enough to run me off of the love for sports, my dislike for being blistering hot and sweaty, but it didn't.

You didn't ask, but I'm gonna tell you anyway. My favorite sport is soccer. Arsenal is my team of choice in the English Premiere League. A close second, a more lifelong viewing sports fan, is American football. The Atlanta Falcons are my team, even if they tend to break my heart at some point every season. I tried to break up with them in the 2013–2014 season to cheer for the team in Nashville, Tennessee Titans, but I just couldn't do it. My heart is red-and-black, for the Falcons and my beloved Georgia Bulldogs.

Before the 2015–2016 season started, my dad and I got to go to the Atlanta Falcons training camp for a day; and if I wasn't a superfan before that (which I probably was), I certainly am now. I spoke at an event in Atlanta in the spring, and then a sweet girl who works for the team offered for me and someone else to be her guests at training camp at the end of the summer. So when I got to pick a plus-one, it was an easy choice of who was going with me. Obviously, Dad. I could not imagine anything cooler. We got to hear from the coaches and see the players practice and stand right on the sidelines of the field. I don't think I stopped smiling for the rest of the day.

Football really is the sport I have grown up loving. Soccer is the one I played, but football is the one I watched. As a high schooler I was the manager of the football team at Sprayberry High School. Yep, that means I spent every week of football season doing sweaty-boy laundry, cleaning up practice equipment, making sure the water coolers were always full, and then the other managers and I would spend Thursday afternoons taking steel wool to every helmet to shine up the gold before the big game on Friday.

But those guys weren't my friends. Of course, I told myself they were because, hello, I wanted to be cool, but I didn't hang out with them outside of school and the field. I didn't text with them or talk with them on the phone. One player came over to my house one night, but that was just because he had asked me to hold a note from his girlfriend before practice and forgot to get it back from me. So he came over to pick it up. They weren't my people, I didn't listen to them talk about their hearts and minds and motivation. (Do high school boys talk about that stuff to anybody? Possibly.)

But then a group of athletes came into my life in 2011, fifteen years later, and those young men did let me hear what was in their minds and hearts.

I remember seeing them as they walked into our college ministry service, the Cross Point Church Nashville Campus, in December 2011. Five young men, standing side by side, and they looked like massive soldiers. They were all easily over six feet tall, and they were thick and solid. I didn't want to fight any of them because I knew I would lose.

I guessed they were athletes, based on their Vanderbilt baseball sweatshirts. I guessed they were country, based on the light-wash Wranglers and boots. They introduced themselves: Connor was the tall blonde that looked like a Ken doll, Keenan was the tan one with the chiseled face of a superhero. Joel had a buzz cut and seemed shy; Andrew introduced himself like a politician with the smile of a celebrity, and Will wore khakis, had floppy blonde hair, and a suspicious smile. I loved them immediately in the way you love people you want to hang on to forever.

That baseball season, 2012, I spent a lot of time around the table with these guys as our friendship grew, and I became the surrogate big sister to these five and a handful of other players. I listened as they talked about girls (A LOT), baseball, school, and God. I heard them when they talked about what it was like to be an athlete, on the good days and the bad, and I heard something I had never heard before.

They didn't believe in quitting.

You know me. My brain does not work like that. But across the board, every athlete I spoke to told me the same thing—they do not quit. Even after the worst games for Vanderbilt, which are few and far between, none of my boys walked off the field and never returned. The home run king would strike out every at-bat in a game, but he didn't quit. The pitcher would get taken out after two innings because of his poor throws, but he didn't quit. The second baseman would make an error, but he didn't throw his glove and rip off his jersey and leave the ballpark. When they won the national championship in 2014, they didn't drop the mic and never return to the field because they had won everything they needed to win. The athletes I know do not know how to quit.

I was curious, and it started a new theory in my mind. Whether it is nature or nurture or a combination of both, why was an athletic brain so different from my own?

I texted my friend Tim to see if we could meet for coffee. As a standout football player at Penn State and then in the NFL, playing for multiple teams over his seven-season career (most recently the Tennessee Titans!), he's the most athletic athlete I know. And about two years ago, he was diagnosed with ALS.

I didn't know Tim Shaw personally before he had ALS, but since I've known him, I've watched him fight and get loud about the disease, about his desire to beat it, and what that is going to look like for him. Even as his body changes in response to the disease—his strength deteriorates, his hands struggle to grasp things at times, his legs don't hold up under him with the same reliability they used to—he remains positive and upbeat and yet truthful and realistic.

And to be honest, it doesn't make any sense to me. When do you just give up? It's the kind of question quitters ask, I realize. But it is what came to my mind as I parked my car and hopped out, headed toward Tim waiting for me outside the coffee shop.

We met at Steadfast Coffee, and I made him try an almond milk chai even though he totally didn't like it. I wanted Tim to tell me about quitting. I wanted to understand his perspective, to see how he could have any hope after such a devastating and life-changing diagnosis. We talked about football; we talked about his upbringing. He furrowed his brow in confusion when I talked about being a quitter, like it was a word he barely recognized. I laughed then because my native tongue of quitting is a foreign language to a guy like Tim. I almost had to explain to him what I meant.

"You know," I said, "it's just like when a workout at the gym is too hard and I don't think I can finish, I quit." And in my mind I pictured pull-ups—because seriously, I cannot do them.

"No," he responded, "when the weights in the gym are too heavy to lift, you can stop for that day, but you go back the next. And you try again. You keep trying to lift until you are able to do it."

It's almost like we defined *quitting* differently. And, in a lot of ways, we defined *grace* differently too. One mistake, one broken link in a chain, and I'm out. I'm done. I've failed. I quit. Tim taught me the difference between pausing and quitting.

And then Tim talked about his mind and the battle there. The heavy lifting, if you will, of what goes on in the mind of an athlete whose body knew few limits until a disease began to eat away at his strength.

His speech doesn't slur, but it struggles, so you have to listen closely as Tim works to make his voice and throat muscles do what he wants them to do when he talks. It is heartbreaking and hope-filled at the same time. We talked for about an hour, all about quitting and not quitting and what strength actually looks like.

I had one more thing I wanted to ask him that felt a little off-limits, a little out-of-bounds. But as I've watched his physical abilities change, as he is able to do less for himself, and when

I read the stats and what is a possible outcome for Tim, I just wondered . . .

"Tim," I asked hesitantly, "at what point do you quit? When do you give up?"

He just stared at me. "I won't quit, Annie."

And I believed him. He won't quit because athletes don't walk away. I see it in him, the mental toughness to be a finisher, and I see it in my Vandybros. They may pause, they may rest, but they don't give up. I thought athletes were stronger than everyone else, but I'm beginning to think they just get grace better than I do. Grace to grow, grace to make mistakes and recover, grace to try again.

I want to be like Tim. I want to erase *quitting* from my dictionary of life and add a little more grace.

But there is no way to tie a neat bow on the end of this. Tim doesn't know how his body will continue to respond and what his physical strength will be day to day. But he still volunteers at church as a greeter, still smiles when he sees me, still asks if I'm ever going to finish writing this chapter about him.

He's not quitting. He's not giving up. He's full of grace towards himself and others. He has taught me that to pause is to win and to rest can actually be a part of the victory. Tim is winning, I'm proud to be his friend. (And yes, Tim, I finally finished writing about you. Hope you like it. And you really need to give almond milk chai another chance.)

LOOK FOR LOVELY

Maybe the best thing you can do today is pause? Maybe you need a break on something, a little rest? You've been trying to finish a project around the house—maybe take a thirty-minute break to play outside? You've been training for a marathon—maybe you should get a massage this week? Remember the mind of an athlete teaches us that to keep from quitting, you have to pause.

THE SOUND OF MUSIC

Cast all your anxiety on him
because he cares for you.

—1 PETER 5:7 NIV

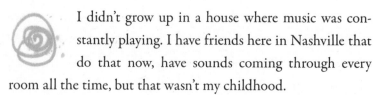

I didn't grow up in a house where music was constantly playing. I have friends here in Nashville that do that now, have sounds coming through every room all the time, but that wasn't my childhood.

I always loved music. I was in choir for my entire childhood and teen life, the highlight being in 1989 when I played Little Psalty in our church's children's musical. Psalty was a singing hymnal that taught children about God, and in one particular scene we meet the young version of him.

Yes. Little Psalty is a boy. But I would not let my art be confined by gender roles! ☺ I slapped that baseball cap on my head and swung the bat over my shoulder and—wearing a cardboard box painted like a hymnal, held on to my body with suspenders—I walked up on stage. There I belted out a few lines of the old hymn "Take My Life and Let It Be." The crowd roared in applause, as much as two hundred parents can roar. But it was, and remains, an absolute highlight of third grade.

I used a hymnal given to me that year by my church choir director, Kibbie DeJarnett, to teach myself to play piano. I knew how to read music enough to read the treble clef line, and I had a beginner's piano book to learn the notes on the keyboard. I would spend hours in my room, with my tiny three-octave keyboard, playing my favorite hymns from church.

But even before that, I remember wearing my ballet tutu at my grandparents' house and dancing around to Burl Ives singing "Lavender Blue."

Probably like you, I can connect just about any year of my life to a song or a musical experience that has been a part of me.

Ben Rector's album *Into the Morning* was in my earbuds through the subways and cab rides of my first full-week visit to New York City in 2010.

I will always think of the Vineyard Music album called *If You Say Go* when I think of my senior year of college. I made all the big decisions with those songs in my head.

Matt Wertz sang "Capitol City" my whole drive to Nashville, when I decided to move in 2008.

As I drove to teach elementary school every morning for five school years, I sang "Legacy" by Nichole Nordeman as a prayer over my students.

Can you do that, too? Link songs or albums or musical experiences to particular seasons of your life?

My high school did musicals, and since I had joined the chorus instead of continuing to play the French horn after middle school (one of my few life regrets because how cool would I be right now if I could play the French horn?), I got to be in the *Sound of Music*, which was amazing. It didn't put in me a longing to chase a Broadway dream to 42nd Street in New York, but I absolutely loved the experience, the darkness of the room and the music soaring through the crowd.

I went to see a few musicals (done by professionals, not the Sprayberry High School chorus) as I was growing up, but it wasn't until college that I had a breathtaking experience around the sounds and the sights and the feel of musical theater.

Some friends had told me about *Les Misérables*, and I had seen the music performed on a PBS special on television, so I knew a lot of the words. I watched that special any time it came on, and in fact, I had recorded it so I could watch it whenever it came to mind. The musical was being performed at the Fox Theater, a beautiful theater in the heart of downtown Atlanta. Ten or so of us bought tickets together—the cheapest seats we could find, sitting in the back row of the balcony—and we drove the ninety miles from the University of Georgia for it.

I didn't know the whole story, just the songs. And as I watched, and the revolt broke out on stage, and characters died heartbreaking deaths, and those scenes mixed with these beautiful songs and lyrics, tears came to my eyes. I don't remember experiencing music that big before—the voices, the large orchestra. All of it almost overwhelmed my senses and left my jaw ajar that such a beautiful experience was wrapped in song.

I saw the power of music that night in a way I had never seen outside of church.

Now I'm addicted to musicals. If they are playing in Nashville, I want to attend. But when I'm in New York City, it is absolutely a must-do. In fact, just last week, my dear friend Jonathan and I went to see *Finding Neverland* on Broadway. It is a movie I have long loved because I love Johnny Depp and I love Peter Pan and so the movie was an instant classic for me. As soon as I heard of the musical, and that Matthew Morrison, Broadway star and Mr. Schuester on the television show *Glee*, would be starring in it, I texted Jonathan. He lives in New York, so I often tend to send him, "NEXT TIME I AM IN NEW YORK WE MUST . . ." texts. I had done that with this musical, that we MUST see it together next time I was in New York. And being the faithful friend he is, he turned down other offers and waited until I arrived in New York City to see it.

We bought matinee tickets the morning of the show, and lucked out getting tickets toward the center just about ten rows back. We had full view of the stage, and I smiled from ear to ear the moment we sat down. The lights dimmed and the curtain parted and I was in awe for the next two hours. The music was beautiful, the performances were incredibly strong, and I won't ruin the ending for you, but I will expose Jonathan and say that we were both WEEPY for the last half hour of the show. It was just unreal. And moving. And I wanted to see it again the next day. Or at least sit in the dark theater with my eyes closed and listen to it all over again.

What is it about music that does that to us? Country music songs, like Clint Black's "State of Mind," talk about it—how a song can take us back to a place, to a memory. But I also think music heals something in us—it soothes, it blesses, it covers. I think our brains and our bodies know how to collect moments like that. According to an article in *Psychology Today*, there is a lot of science behind the connection between sounds and memories.[3] I feel that in me, and I feel what happens when music binds up something that feels like it has fallen to pieces inside of me.

Maybe that's why David wrote so many psalms. Maybe for him, just like for me with Psalty songs, there's a connection that he craved as an adult, and he found it in the sounds of his childhood. The songs he sang as a shepherd boy, maybe those are the same ones that rang through the castle when he was king. Because there is comfort there, don't you agree?

Last year, as God built perseverance in me and cleaned my soul of the broken crazy, my days were particularly marked by a few albums on repeat in my head and heart. From January through the spring, it was all Bethel Music's *We Will Not Be Shaken*. The third track, "Jesus We Love You," became my airplane song, the one I would play anytime we were high above the clouds. The spring and summer switched to Hillsong United's *Empires*. My life season switched as well; I went from being in a place where I felt like God was advancing things to a summer of waiting and watching and trusting and wondering. And that album held me through it.

I think something shifts in my head and heart and atmosphere when worship is playing. Most mornings when I'm getting ready, I will play whatever album I'm addicted to currently—right now it's Amanda Cook's *Brave New World*—and let the music play through my Apple TV so that it fills the house. My day starts different when it starts like that.

You may laugh at me, but I clearly remember the first worship music I ever bought. Until I was in high school, I didn't know that you could own the songs we listened to in church. I mean, we obviously had kid Christian music like Psalty, but I didn't have any grown-up stuff until my senior year of high school. At a winter retreat called In the Vine, the worship band sold their CDs outside the meeting room. I bought one for $5 and immediately went back to my bunk to listen to it. For the entire free time, three hours, I lay on the top bunk by the window and listened to that five-song CD over and over again, amazed that I could actually own it myself. The songs that moved me to tears in the worship center were now in my ears.

I know, that's almost laughable now when we can hear a song on television and own it on our iPhone in less than a minute, but in high school? It blew my mind. And it changed my life. I filled my home life and car life with worship music after that retreat. It was the sea I swam through.

The summer after my sophomore year of college, I was a youth group intern, but about three weeks in, the youth pastor left and took a full-time pastoring job. Suddenly this fun part-time job with a youth pastor I loved being around became my full-time full-stress lonely job. The students, parents, and church were awesome. It was just that I was twenty. I had no idea how to run an entire youth group—to meet all their spiritual needs as well as their fun youth group summer hangout needs.

I worked really hard. And I went home every night and practically melted down. The stress to please and to create and to organize was more than I felt I could handle.

So every night around 10:00 p.m., I would watch *Mary Poppins*.

Yep. The whole thing. I usually fell asleep with twenty or so minutes left, but every night I watched it. There was something about the simplicity of the story and the connection to my childhood and the music. It all combined to be the force that kept me getting up and going back to work the next day.

I would cry, often, when Julie Andrews sang "Stay Awake" to help the Banks children fall asleep. It felt like she was taking care of me, protecting me, wishing me well. I know that sounds kind of ludicrous, but it was what worked and was balm for my soul. It was the moment I collected; it was the lovely I found in a life where stress was thrown at me suddenly. And the music would reverberate through my mind all day long.

I'm not a musically talented person, though I wish I were. (I sing like I think I'm a great singer.) I taught myself to play the piano as a kid. I learned French horn in middle school. I learned the guitar in college because I was a Christian in college, and that kind of feels like a spiritual rite of passage, know what I mean? But I'm not stellar in any of the instruments. I live in a town full of people who play instruments for a living, who feel about music the way I feel about words on pages, who have found a calling and a ministry in song. That's not me, but I'm thankful those people exist because they are the ones who make the music that moves me. I'm not the kind who listens for certain chords and notes and such, but when a song resonates with me, I don't forget it.

Just this week, I was FaceTiming with my friends Matthew and Brittany as they were putting their children to bed. The last thing they do is sing together and pray; and as we were all sitting there, their oldest, Parker, started to sing . . .

"I caaaast all my caaaares upon Youuuuu, I laaaaay all of my burdens down at Your feet. And anytiiiime I don't knoooow, wha-at to do, I will caaaaast all my caaaares upon Youuu."[4]

And as I listened to her, my mind took me back to the bedroom of my childhood, memories flooded of learning to play the piano and singing along to every Psalty record. I was reminded that I knew that song in a time when I worried a lot. Constantly. And when I couldn't fall asleep, or when I woke up and felt panic or sick to my stomach, that's the song I would sing. I started to sing along with her, thinking of my day and my own worries and what was going on in my life; and after we hung up, I was still singing. And praying. And remembering all the times God really did take my cares upon Himself and let me rest.

That's what music does. It holds you together when you think you'll fall apart. It reminds you of truth. It grabs your hand as you try to cross the finish line. It fills your ears with peace when it feels like there is no peace.

LOOK FOR LOVELY

Ask your friends or your social media network and find a new worship album to download. And when you buy it, listen all the way through.

NAIL POLISH

Your beauty should not come from outward adornment, such as elaborate hairstyles and the wearing of gold jewelry or fine clothes. Rather, it should be that of your inner self, the unfading beauty of a gentle and quiet spirit, which is of great worth in God's sight.

—1 PETER 3:3–4 NIV

 My hands don't look like kid hands anymore. They don't look bad or weird or ugly; they just don't look young anymore. Getting older is a weird thing. In a Western culture that teaches that beauty is found in youth, the process of slowly seeing that fade away is interesting and different from what I would have predicted.

Jordan was with me when I found my first gray hair. It was while I was working at the Mocha Club and she was working at FASHIONABLE, and the two companies shared an office. I passed by a mirror and noticed an off-colored hair sticking up from the part at the crown of my head. I grabbed it, held on to it, and ran out to her, sitting at a table surrounded by colorful scarves.

"JORDAN, WHAT IS THIS."

It was more a statement in panic than a question. Jordan, seven or so years younger than me, changed her face from shock to sympathy. And I knew.

"I think it's a gray hair, Annie."

Yes. Yes it was. I plucked that puppy out and swore I would continue to rid my head of these. I would not give up the fight to maintain my mousey brown coif. It was merely a matter of months before they multiplied like rabbits, and suddenly the decision to pluck them was going to contribute to a possible balding problem. So now they sit, atop my head, declaring to the world that I am no longer the teen I once was.

Except when it comes to my fingernails. While my hands most assuredly look like the hands of a mid-thirty-year-old woman, my fingernails are painted with all the accoutrements of your average seventeen-year-old gal.

I see my hands a lot. It's a part of the job, the fact that I type all day every day. So my hands sit right here, in front of my face. A neon yellow is my current nail polish color of choice. I find the bright colors to be my favorite, even though they can be mildly (or mostly) distracting. Each of my ring fingers is painted with the neon yellow and silver glitter on top. Yes, I am channeling my inner '80s child this week. But I like seeing the brightness and the sparkle dance across my keyboard as I type. It speaks of deeper things to me. An outward sign of a healthy heart.

I have been a nail-biter most of my life. As an elementary-age student, I bit and picked at my nails until they bled. I bit my nails when I was nervous. I bit my nails when I was bored. I bit my nails when I was sad, lonely, busy, scared. It really didn't matter. I bit them down until you could see the tips peeled to deeper levels and the nail bed would be revealed on each finger. It was ugly.

As a teenager I continued the habit. The idea of having pretty nails never crossed my mind. Why would I focus on such tiny details when the big picture was hopeless? Is changing the light switches in a room really going to do all that much to cover up the hideous wallpaper?

While still living in Marietta, however, I started to join friends at the nail salon more often. As the Lord was healing my mind, I slowly attempted to defeat the habit and try to keep a color of some sort on my hands. Biting my nails was a habit that needed to be broken. Bottles of "stop biting" nail polish piled up in my bathroom drawers. After a bad day, I would revert to biting my nails again and then begin the process all over again. In time the old habit died with the old mind-set, but I still would pick at and mess with my nails when I was having emotional struggles. By the time I moved to Nashville, the paint on the nails was the first to go, versus having my hands in my mouth and biting until they were throbbing with pain.

Now the habit is almost (almost!) defeated. It's a superrare, supernervous day that my nails take a hit.

During the broken crazy season of my life, I sat down to breakfast with my friend Sonnie at Star Bagel in Sylvan Park. We were just catching up with life, having not seen each other for a while. As I picked up my breakfast to eat, Sonnie noticed that not only were my nails not painted, but they were tiny, red, wounded.

"Oh my gosh, Annie, your nails!," she said surprised. "What happened?"

I looked down, having not even realized how they looked. Wow. What an outward reflection of an inward pain. I started to tell her everything, where things felt wrong, where the broken crazy had originated, and what I was trying to do to stand up to it, what it felt like when I failed to do so.

I realized that day that my fingernails had become a gauge of sorts. Painted and manicured, all is well. Bare but shaped well, I'm too busy. Bitten down and gross, we've got a problem.

But now it's even more than just a good indicator of my personal and mental health. I find strength in the beauty. Though my hands are aging, along with the creases beside my eyes and the gray hairs poking through, they have been kind to me. It's when I am able to hold on when I wanted to let go, when words go down on paper, or I'm able to lift more grocery bags than I think—that's when I realize my hands are part of the solution to finding beauty, not part of the problem.

So I take my nail polish situation pretty seriously. Which may sound silly to you, and I'm okay with that. But that's the thing about looking for lovely around you—what you find beautiful may not be what I find beautiful. The moments you collect that will help you finish the thing you've started may not be moments that matter to me.

Oh the beauty of being humans who are allowed to be creatively different, yes?

So I paint my nails. Depending on my mood and the weather and the season and the event. Sometimes it is the new gel shellac situation that can last for a few weeks, but at the rate I like to change colors, gel is usually reserved for international trips or weddings. I'm about half-and-half getting my nails painted at the salon versus painting them myself at home. My personal nail polish collection has grown significantly as people have gifted me lots of bottles, many of them containing glitter. Which, clearly, is a joy to my heart. So I love laying all the shades out and picking the one that is right for the moment and right for the day. (Yes, sometimes I can change daily. I'm so annoying like that.)

Winter brings shades of chestnut and mocha, a personal favorite color being You Don't Know Jacque from OPI. Autumn I love a good gray or a mauve, like my grandmother used to wear. Spring I prefer the light pinks, light gray with sparkles, or Easter egg colors. And summer? It has become my favorite. Brights. Hot pink. White. Orange. Anything that screams "Beach! Laughter! Tan! Fruit! Outside!"

First Peter 3:3–4 speaks of not focusing too much on your outward appearance. It was a warning, at the time, to the women of Israel to not become like the Egyptian women and spend hours focused on outer beauty. Instead, Peter says, spend time on who you are on the inside.

I used to not like these verses. (Am I allowed to say that?) It didn't resonate with me because I thought about all the time I spent in church and all the time I spent trying to be the "right person," but I never felt like I had a gentle spirit, and I continued to hate my body. But what I have learned of late is that when I focused on the inside, the outside changed, too. The focus isn't on clocking time with God just for the sake of checking off your daily responsibilities. "Did I pray today? Did I read my Bible? Did I journal? Okay, then I'm good!" I tried that for a long time. I thought that was building my strength. But it wasn't. When I am doing the hard work of healing for my soul, when I am letting God dig down into the hurt places and expose them and heal them, my body responds with health as well. But when my inside is neglected and hurting, it shows in my hands and in my eyes. Not in the crow's-feet, but in the sadness that can't be denied when someone looks right at me. I am never quiet (if I'm awake), but my spirit can be quiet. My heart can be at rest. And my painted nails will prove that to you.

What in your life paints the picture of the health of your soul? You know those verses I used to not love? Well, 1 Peter 3:3 tells us what beauty should not consist of but is quickly followed by verse 4 telling us beauty "should consist of what is inside the heart with the imperishable quality of a gentle and quiet spirit." I love how Scripture leaves us with this true beauty that will last forever. It doesn't mean I'm going to stop painting my nails or working out or brushing my hair—all activities that make me feel good about myself and help me see lovely. It just means that I notice those things for what they are, put them in their appropriate spot behind the focus of a healthy soul and spirit, and continue to run toward that health.[5]

LOOK FOR LOVELY

Paint your nails today! Whether it is your first time EVER (start with a pink!) or you are addicted like me (add a signature nail!), today is the day for a little manicure. As you are painting, use it as a time to pray and ask God what it would look like for you to cultivate a quiet and gentle spirit, to find for yourself what is health for your soul and your body.

SUSHI

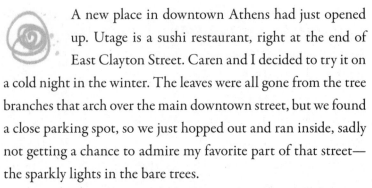

For God is not a God of disorder but of peace.

—1 CORINTHIANS 14:33 NIV

A new place in downtown Athens had just opened up. Utage is a sushi restaurant, right at the end of East Clayton Street. Caren and I decided to try it on a cold night in the winter. The leaves were all gone from the tree branches that arch over the main downtown street, but we found a close parking spot, so we just hopped out and ran inside, sadly not getting a chance to admire my favorite part of that street— the sparkly lights in the bare trees.

It was a big-deal adult dinner for us. No longer college students (by approximately five months), we were going out to dinner during the week to speak of our work woes and the challenges of being OH SO MATURE AND ADULT. So clearly we needed sushi because that's what all the twenty-three-year-old working gals in the big city were eating tonight too.

Neither of us really knew how to order. Southern gals like us can hold our own in a barbecue restaurant or in a meat-and-three place, but this sushi business was way out of our comfort zone. I read the menu and looked at the pictures. I had seen sushi before obviously but had never tasted it. So I didn't know what any of the rolls were going to be like. There was lots I didn't know about this particular experience. I didn't know how much sushi I needed to call it a meal, but I was betting it was more than one roll. I wasn't sure what I would like and what I wouldn't like, though I was pretty certain raw-ness was not going to be my favorite. (This is a problem, as you probably know, because 90 percent of sushi rolls are raw.)

I also didn't know what the seaweed paper was going to do to my intestines. Ahem.

So we ordered to the best of our uneducated ability. We got edamame; that seemed understandable enough. Healthy, simple, not mixed with raw ocean animals. At the waitress's suggestion, I got two rolls that night, one with crab and one with shrimp. I didn't love the taste of the seaweed, but the rest of the sushi experience was awesome.

But for the next two days, everything smelled and tasted like seaweed, and my stomach turned anytime I thought of it. Eventually, I was WHOA REALLY sick and never returned to the land of seaweed eating. In fact, I swore off sushi after that one experience in my college town because I was certain it was altogether poisonous.

That was until I moved to Nashville and told the story to my Bible study group. "No, no, no," Graham said, "let us take you to Samuri Sushi. It's the best in town, and you don't even have to have seaweed. You can ask for soy paper wraps instead."

I couldn't believe it. For years I had been avoiding sushi because of the seaweed, and now there was another option. We went, and I let Graham and Hillary order for me. A few minutes later out came the most beautiful plate of food I had ever seen. The Hawaiian roll was spread out on the plate, the pale soy paper wrapped around rice and fried shrimp, asparagus, and topped with mango and peanuts. I had died and gone to Asian food heaven. The second roll they had ordered for me was the Happy Roll, similar to the Hawaiian but with crab and asparagus inside and kiwi on top.

The plate was so colorful. Reds and oranges, whites and greens. It looked like something that was drawn with big fat markers from your elementary school classroom.

And since that day in 2008, sushi has become a staple in my dietary life. I am still the wimpiest of all sushi eaters, leaning more toward shrimp and crab rolls, none of that raw salmon business, and certainly I steer clear from the scoop of fish eggs they can spread across the top of the rolls. But you can talk me into sushi just about any night of the week.

One night Nichole texted to see if I wanted Ginza for dinner, the small local sushi spot just around the corner from our houses. I didn't even have to answer. I just asked how quickly she could get there because, yes, sushi was calling my name for dinner, that was for sure.

I pretty much wanted to be anywhere but at my house that night. Just weeks after returning from the beach trip where I had run from Matt to stare my broken crazy in the face, I was now back home, and though I was seeing a counselor, I couldn't seem to pull my life together. I washed clothes and left them in the dryer, just plucking from there when something I wanted to wear was still hanging out in there. I used all the dishes, leaving dirty ones in the sink. I attempted to clean out some clothes and purge a bit, thinking a fresh start would help my mind, but it mainly just led to piles of clothes on the floor that I stepped over on the way to my bed every night. (I lived alone at the time—did I mention that? So I wasn't ruining anyone else's life but my own.)

So I had been there, in the messiest house, all day already, lying on the couch, watching television. It started innocently enough with a Men's World Cup soccer match that morning. Then I fell asleep, got up and had lunch, then was back on the couch, watching a movie. I felt like I blinked and it was dinnertime. In reality I watched about ten hours of television. So I was ready to breathe some fresh air, eat something besides Honey Nut Chex, and see a human.

Nichole and I sat down in the first green booth on the left when you walk in the door of Ginza. We were both wearing shorts, as it was one hundred degrees outside, the dog days of a southern summer, so our bare legs stuck to the plastic booths. Hardly having to look at the menu, we ordered our usual—edamame to share, one roll and a bowl of white rice for her, two rolls for me.

We talked about normal things. I mentioned none of my broken crazy or how I had spent my entire day lying on the couch. She told me about her business and a phone call with her mom. I sat there pretty quiet, just trying to glaze over all the things I was feeling but didn't have a category for. As she spoke, we ate through the edamame, the peas popping easily out of their salty pods.

Within a few minutes the rolls (and rice) were delivered to the table, and our waiter refilled the water glasses we had both emptied. I looked down at my two rolls, and without warning, my eyes were blurred with tears.

They were beautiful. And orderly. And colorful. And natural.

I saw God in those sushi rolls. I saw how He is a God who puts everything in its right place.

For God is not a God of disorder but of peace. (1 Cor. 14:33)

Each piece of the roll was symmetrical. There wasn't anything artificial in there. It was all real and orderly, and it made me cry because I saw the lovely, and I wanted it in my life. It felt like God whispered something into my heart about seeing how He does things and trying to be like Him. He wasn't out to shame my broken crazy or make me feel like I was a bad person. I think He just wanted me to see the beauty of order.

I went home after dinner and loaded the dishwasher. Then I folded that one half-load of clothes that had been sitting in the dryer. Don't get it twisted; I didn't do some massive overhaul of my life that night. I just came home and put two rather simple areas of my life in order. One for each roll I had for dinner, I suppose. That tiny bit of lovely set my night on a healthier track.

I pick sushi now on days where things feels out of bounds or when life feels messy because I found what I was looking for there, even if I didn't realize how much I was looking. I found lovely. I found God. I saw Him there and I still do.

I got home from about fifteen days straight of speaking on the road, driving from city to city, and I had one night in Nashville before flying to Austin for the If:Gathering. I immediately asked the girls if we could please go to Virago. It's way too fancy for a normal sushi dinner (that's why we have Ginza), but when a Virago request is made, people understand the situation. This isn't a normal day; this is an especially exciting or especially hard day. And this one felt especially hard. Road life isn't always easy for me, particularly when I feel like I'm missing out on friend time, so this one day when I have literally one meal in town with my friends made my job feel costly, and it made me feel sad, and I felt like life was very messy.

I threw on my glitter flats and met the girls in the Gulch at Virago. They sat us in a booth toward the back, and I sat quietly as my friends caught one another up on their days and dates and dreams. I wasn't trying to be uninvolved; I just wanted to hear them, watch them, be with them; and I wanted to save my voice because I had done a lot of talking lately on stages.

We started with crispy rice spicy tuna, the only almost raw thing I will eat in a sushi restaurant and the actual reason we go to Virago. It's an oval of rice, fried, and then topped with a tiny scoop of spicy raw tuna. Then they set the rolls on watermelon Pop Rocks. HOW WEIRD AND PERFECT IS THAT? We shared that appetizer, but for my main course I ordered The Bomb with soy paper. That roll is so expensive in calories and dollars that I cannot even talk about it. It has crab and shrimp and asparagus (can you sense a theme in my sushi taste?) and gold flakes or something because I have to dip into my savings account anytime I want to eat it. But it is oh.so.worth.it. The taste is near perfection, especially with a few drops of soy sauce. It came out, and I looked at it for a minute before I dug in.

I knew what I needed to see. The order. The colors. The peace. The Pop Rocks. I knew if I looked, I could find lovely in that sushi roll. Every time I order a roll these days, my mind immediately thinks back to Ginza with Nichole and how I saw, for the first time, God using sushi to remind me of His sovereign hand. So on a night like that, just a few hours of being with my girlfriends, just one night in my own bed, the sushi brought me peace. God is ordering my steps, God is ordering all things, and I rest in that.

LOOK FOR LOVELY

If you've never tried sushi, TODAY IS YOUR DAY! Go big and raw and fishy or don't and sushi like me. But tonight for dinner, why not grab a roll or two? But before you eat it, look at it. Really look at it. See the colors and the symmetry and the way it is beautiful. Maybe God wants to remind you of something in that roll tonight.

b.fab.fitness

Now the Lord is the Spirit, and where
the Spirit of the Lord is, there is freedom.

—2 CORINTHIANS 3:17 NIV

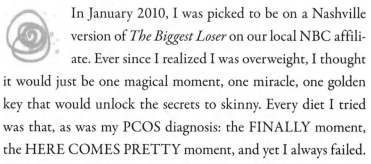 In January 2010, I was picked to be on a Nashville version of *The Biggest Loser* on our local NBC affiliate. Ever since I realized I was overweight, I thought it would just be one magical moment, one miracle, one golden key that would unlock the secrets to skinny. Every diet I tried was that, as was my PCOS diagnosis: the FINALLY moment, the HERE COMES PRETTY moment, and yet I always failed.

But surely being challenged to lose weight on television would be the trick. This time there was no secret to it—all my friends would see and know, as would a few hundred thousand viewers across Middle Tennessee. And that accountability was bound to make my body behave and my mind toughen up.

"Don't embarrass yourself by failing at this, Downs," I would say to myself at practically every meal, "Every unmarried man in this town is watching." Also I'm competitive. So when there were twelve of us but only one person could be the losiest loser of them all, I was bound and determined it would be me.

What did you win? Besides Nashville fame and glory from the midday news show watchers?

A year's supply of Subway sandwiches. And a gym membership.

(The prizes were legit, but I wanted bragging rights the most. Definitely more than I wanted a year of six-inch subs.)

One of the problems with the Get Fit Challenge, as it is called, was that I had to exercise a lot. They were keeping track of that; we had all received a free membership to a local gym for the duration of the competition—approximately four months. The television cameras would want to follow us around; the trainers and producers wanted to see our stats and would check in weekly.

Ever since my soccer career came to a glorious end with a torn MCL my senior year of high school, exercise has been a chore, not a choice. I knew my body would like it if I got consistent, but I didn't want to do that. It was always painful and took up my time; and because my hair sweats first, it meant a lot of hair washing when I was in one of those "seasons of self-improvement." So my habit had been to go to a gym once a week, halfheartedly do the elliptical, and then check EXERCISE off on the to-do sheet of my life. But during this competition? They wanted me to exercise every day, but I knew no exercise that I liked, much less loved enough to fit it into my everyday.

A few weeks into the competition, I had lost approximately two pounds, which was about eighteen pounds less than I wanted to lose the first month. (Unrealistic expectations? Clearly.) The trainer in charge of our fitness planned a Saturday Zumba-thon for us.

I did not know what Zumba was in 2010, much less what it meant to attend a Zumba-thon. But it was required as it would be that week's episode of the Get Fit Challenge, so all the contestants had to show up and show out and Zumba.

I invited a bunch of friends because I thought it was pretty fun to get my friends television time, and it made the whole thing less a competition show and more an almost-Annie-Downs-reality-show, and I was all about that. So about ten of us showed up at this gym on the west side of Nashville early on a Saturday morning, ready to try this Zumba thing.

If you don't know what Zumba is, much as I didn't, it is a workout class where you dance to Latin music. Lots of hip swirling and clapping and fast footwork. I started out slow and hesitant, watching the moves more than doing them, but as the Zumba-thon went on that day (which just meant it was lots of hours of Zumba where the teachers switch out and the students keep going), I began to enjoy it. A few hours in, I pulled our Get Fit Challenge trainer aside.

"Where else can I do this?" I asked her. "Is this a thing? Does this actually count as exercise?"

"This is exactly the exercise you need to do, just because you asked that question." Was her response.

And it was a lightbulb moment for me. I prioritize fun; I want to be having fun almost always if not always, and exercise had always interrupted that. But suddenly I had found an activity that someone else was categorizing as exercise but I was calling fun.

It was like I had just located and captured a unicorn.

I got home that afternoon and looked at my local YMCA group exercise schedule, and sure enough, there were four or five Zumba classes every week! How had I missed this? Immediately, I started adjusting my daily work schedule (the perk of being my own boss) and let my girlfriends know where the party was. Within a few days a handful of us were showing up to the Y for Zumba every time they let us. It was the fullness of joy for me; I was getting better at the moves, my friends were there, and this was EXERCISE?! What a treat!

I went to the YMCA south of Nashville once alone for a class. I was usually a neighborhood YMCA kind of gal, but the way my schedule worked that day and when the class was offered and the fact I (gasp) wanted to go made it so it was just me and this unfamiliar location. It had been a long day of writing, trying to finish up telling some of the harder stories in my first book, *Perfectly Unique*. I was pretty emotionally spent. The teacher was a tiny blonde girl that I was certain, at some point, had been an NFL cheerleader. The class was packed to the gills with middle-aged white women, so I slinked into the back left corner, getting a little place for me and sliding my towel, keys, and water bottle against the wall.

We started with songs I knew, moves that had become familiar to me, so I started to dance. And sweat. And cry.

It was almost an out-of-body experience. I could feel myself crying as Shakira sang about Africa and we spun around with our arms out like an airplane. It's a great song—"Waka Waka (This Time for Africa)"—it was the theme for the 2010 World Cup hosted by South Africa. But while I spun around and cried, I also was trying to listen to my heart.

What was going on?

What were these tears about?

I've cried while exercising before, so that's nothing new. But usually it's because I hated what I was doing, and that wasn't what I was feeling now. I loved what we were doing.

I realized I felt free. When I was spinning around and stomping and jumping, I felt like a kid, and I felt released from the pain and struggle of the work I had done that day.

This was a new experience for me. Exercise making me feel good? Exercise clearing my mind and setting me free? I didn't know anything about this. But I knew I loved it.

(By the way, I didn't win the Get Fit Challenge. I lost around eleven pounds in the four months, which was nothing compared to the winner who lost more than thirty! Whah whah. I'm a loser. The wrong kind. I'm sorry I let you down. And this wasn't a golden key to the life of loving me I so desperately longed for after all.)

Even when the competition ended, I continued to do Zumba. I didn't go every day, but I kept it as a once- or twice-a-week exercise because I loved it. And I couldn't believe I loved it.

That fall Lyndsay sent a text to a handful of us that were Zumba-ing together about a new class in town called b.fab.fitness. It cost $3 to attend, so it was right in the budget of what I was willing to spend on exercise. It met at a gym in a different part of town than where we usually hung out, but it was safe and was supposedly really fun.

We showed up at the Coleman Community Center the next Monday night for the 7:00 p.m. class. We each paid our $3 and walked into the gym. We were five minutes early, but the gym was already almost full. There were probably two hundred women there, and it looked like every cultural, economic, and racial subgroup was represented. Some of the women had on jeans and T-shirts; others wore fancy Lulu Lemon workout clothes, and a few had on jingly belts like a belly dancer would wear. And the teacher was a DUDE. What was the world into which we had just entered?

The class was called b.fab.fitness, and from what I had read on the website, it was similar to Zumba but would be using hip-hop/top 40 music instead of Latin music.

And so it was. The bass of the first song kicked in, and all the women, led by again—A DUDE, started dancing like crazy, whooping and hollering, and just absolutely having a blast. Within minutes I was one of them. Dancing. Laughing. Clapping. Hollering. We sang along to some radio hits and shook our hips and kicked our legs and punched the air and did a few body rolls, just for good measure. The hour class flew by. It was over before I even had time to check the clock! And I was sweating like crazy, my pedometer telling me we had burned almost a thousand calories. I loved Zumba, but I was HOME here.

My confidence level in my own ability to dance had grown significantly through Zumba, and so by the time I was here at b.fab, I was an active participant. Again, it felt like freedom. I felt like with every song and every move, I was shaking off something that was holding me back. And I could feel that God was restoring things to me—confidence in myself and my body, gratitude for how He made me. I felt capable to do what He had called me to do. I liked how, as we continued to go back to b.fab week after week, the moves became familiar to me, and I stopped thinking about them and began even more to feel them, and my mind healed as my body moved.

My counselor loved that I loved b.fab. I loved that I loved b.fab. In a way I can't totally explain, I felt God in that class. Maybe it was the variety of women in there, or the release that the experience brought to my body and heart, but I teared up often in that gym, whether it was processing what I had worked on that day or feeling sadness because something was going wrong in my personal life, it all just sort of worked itself out there on the gym floor. I would talk to God as I danced. I would catch myself praying and listening and communing with God, sometimes while doing a body roll or a grapevine to the right.

I still go to b.fab at least once a week, multiple times if I can fit it in my schedule. I keep a little collection of dollar bills in a jar in my room so that I'm never without the cash I need for the class, in case I decide I want to go at the last minute or my calendar clears. I have my spot where I stand, back left, right on the arch of the three-point shooting line painted on the basketball court floor. Sometimes friends come with me; sometimes they don't. I don't always get to body roll, but every time, without fail, I feel God.

LOOK FOR LOVELY

Listen to Shakira's "Waka Waka" song and give yourself permission to dance a little bit. No pressure, doesn't have to be choreographed or beautiful, just let yourself go to the music—sway, swing, jump, whatever you want. There is no wrong answer here. Just give your body a chance express and release.

MONET'S HOUSE

Live in harmony with
one another.

—ROMANS 12:16 NIV

When I was in the youth group, our church had a family serving as missionaries in the heart of Paris, France. Thanks to them we had the unique opportunity to spend our high school spring break weeks in Paris, partnering with them in ministry and sharing the gospel. We stayed in host homes, we did musical performances around town that told the story of Jesus, and I grew to love Paris. It didn't feel romantic or like home to me; it just always felt comfortable.

I love all the big spots in Paris—Notre Dame, the tiny crepe place just beside Notre Dame, Sacré-Coeur, Montmartre, Versailles and the queen's quarters behind it. The only thing I do not love, and I like to complain about given the chance, is the Louvre.

Now listen. I like art. I really do. And large paintings that span across a room absolutely take my breath away.

But the Louvre? I do not like it. When I was a teenager, they took my book bag from me as I entered, making me "check" it with the coats, leaving me without my water bottle or my camera, and I was fit to be tied, totally undone. And apparently I still hold a grudge many years later. (I should give it another run, probably. But I'm not quite ready to do that yet.)

I also have so much eye roll for the *Mona Lisa*. She's tiny and crowded. You can hardly get up next to her to see her, and once you do, it's like, "Eh, okay, I saw it. What now?" And then her eyes follow you around the room, and it's wicked creepy.

After I graduated high school, my family saved up money, and we took a trip to London and Paris. Sally was just nine or ten. Tatum and I were high schoolers. At this point I had spent three spring breaks in Paris, so returning with my family felt like I was showing them around a town I thought I knew. Our main goal, the big highlight, was hanging out with the DeJarnett family, the ones who were there serving as missionaries.

One day we decided to take a day trip to Giverny, where famous painter Claude Monet's home still stands. My mom is a longtime art fan, and I had grown to love it as well (except for the *Mona Lisa*, obviously), and so I was really excited for this excursion. It was only about an hour's drive from where we were staying in Jouy-en-Josas to Giverny, so we loaded up the rental car and headed northwest, past Versailles, toward the suburb where the house stood.[6]

We arrived, and the line to buy a ticket to tour the home and gardens was twenty or so people deep. Sally had stayed back with the DeJarnetts to ride bikes with their daughter Marie-Claire, so it was just the four of us—Mom, Dad, Tatum, and me. I don't know what the tour is like now, but in 1998 you didn't get to see many rooms, and you could not take any pictures. But I didn't need to—the interior of the house is strong in my memory.

The tour mainly focuses on five or six rooms on the main floor of the home. Monet picked all the paint colors, the tour guide told us, and each was intentional based on the natural light, the wood, and the decor he wanted to put in the room. As the tour guide led us into the dining room, she pointed out the color on the walls. The room was sunny yellow on every wall. Very simple, but two tones of really perfect dining room yellows. It felt like the shades that would set people at ease and feel fresh year round. The glassware in the room, in the china cabinets and all the shelves, was blue. Bright blue.

While we were still standing there, on the rust red-and-white checkered floors, she pointed through the dining room into the kitchen. You could only see through a wide doorway, but the kitchen was a beautiful soft blue. Blue-and-white tiles, plus the natural light coming through the windows that we could not see, combined to give the doorway almost a hazy blue feel. And then when you stand in the blue kitchen and look into the dining room, the brightness of the yellow is so inviting and fun.

It wasn't just about the yellow of the dining room, she explained. It was about the yellow when you can see the blue of the kitchen. It made both colors better, brighter, and more impactful when they were combined. So Monet picked the two colors of these rooms to complement each other and to take what is already lovely and make it even lovelier. A website about the home, created by the city of Giverny, says, "Monet wanted a blue kitchen so that the guests would see the right color in harmony with the yellow dining room when the door to the kitchen was open."[7]

Yes. The harmony. I felt that.

Every color was picked for its own values but also for how it would look in connection with the other rooms around it. I just kept popping back and forth between the two rooms, even after the tour group began to move from the house to the gardens, where the water lilies pond still exists. (And seriously, it looks exactly like Monet's series of water lilies paintings. It's incredible.)

I think about these two rooms all the time, and I've spent significant brain space over the years trying to decorate my home in harmonizing blues and yellows. I can't forget how those colors, while truly beautiful on their own, were actually far more stunning together. Though super different, the way these colors cooperated impacted me.

One of my best friends in Nashville is Nichole. (You didn't miss some transition paragraph that accidentally got deleted. Hang with me, and you'll see the connection between Nichole and Monet.)

Nichole is from the North; Ohio, to be precise. She probably wouldn't call it the north, but where I come from, Ohio is absolutely the North.

(I am from the South.)

Nichole was an elite-level gymnast as a child and still cries when she watches the Olympic Games because she feels so connected to the sport. She was a division one level college athlete in swimming.

(When I was in college, I went to the University of Georgia workout facility about once a month and took bowling as my college physical education class.)

Nichole is a CPA and honors the power of numbers and balance sheets and dollar signs.

(I don't like to live by a budget because I feel like I'm being bullied.)

Nichole is often more quiet and reserved, choosing to listen and ask questions.

(I'm Annie. I'm loud. Always.)

If someone needs a wing woman, if one of us is having to go somewhere alone and wishes we had a friend to go with us,

Nichole is always that girl. It actually doesn't matter to Nichole whether she knows the other people at the event or not. In fact, more often than not, Nichole does not want to go to the event in question, but if one of her friends needs her, she shows up.

(I tend to shy away from doing things I don't want to do. On the selfish scale, I'm on it.)

She doesn't give up. I've watched her struggle with the business she owns, struggle with questions in her faith, struggle with her health, family issues, and hurts. And yet she doesn't give up.

(I'm a quitter.)

We are very different. We share a few things, like our faith and enjoyment of sushi and swimming pools, but if you just looked at the stats, if you just looked at our histories, you would never put us together.

Like blue. And yellow.

But something happens when we stand by each other. My loud brings beauty to her quiet, and her quiet brings beauty to my loud. My selfishness really displays her consistent willingness to be a wing woman, and her generosity really makes my selfishness, um, stand out. Her northernness mixes with my southernness; and though we don't always understand each other's upbringing (WHY DO YOU SAY POP FOR COKE?), I appreciate her shade of culture, and she appreciates mine. We look better together than apart. She adds value to my life, and next to me she makes me a more beautiful Annie.

It's like a body with lots of parts, isn't it? Like it says in 1 Corinthians 12, there is so much benefit from the parts working together. Blue and yellow, Annie and Nichole, an arm and a leg. Our differences are clear, but the ways we can work together far surpass the need to focus on ways we aren't alike.

This is why we can't be friends just with folks who look and act just like us. When I moved to Nashville, I initially set out to make friends with people who reminded me of my friends from home. Similar upbringing, similar college experience, similar faith journey. It's easier that way, to know and be known, just as it is easier to paint two rooms the same shade of blue. But as I met men and women who weren't like me—Nichole is a perfect example—my mind expanded. True faith can look like my life, but it looks like her life too, even though we are different. And it just kept happening—becoming friends with people who are not at all like me. Because of the melting pot of Nashville, and people moving in to this city from every corner of the map, finding someone from metro Atlanta that was also a Georgia Bulldog became less simple and honestly, less important.

It's why, at times, the best thing you can do when you meet someone new is look past all the differences and focus on what you share. Because we don't need to just be like us forever. There are parts of my hue that would improve if I were more like Nichole, and there may be times my friendship helps her as well. But had we looked at each other five years ago when we met and just went with what we saw at first blush, we'd have thought our colors were too different to stand together well. I'm glad we didn't quit then. I'm glad when we saw my blue and her yellow, we didn't walk away and set out for me to find more blues and for her to find more yellows.

Monet's house taught me something valuable that has stuck with me for almost two decades. I see it working in my life and I thank God for Monet, for yellow and blue, and for Nichole.

LOOK FOR LOVELY

Which friend in your life is different from you? Call her today, and thank her for all the ways her uniqueness complements your own. Maybe this is also a good time to make a new friend, someone who seems different from you, someone you have avoided because you were certain the commonalities couldn't override the differences. Younger, older, someone from a different culture, race, or religious background. Make that extra effort to reach out beyond your current circle and get to know that person you've maybe seen or spoken to in passing.

MY PEOPLE

Every time you cross my mind,
I break out in exclamations of
thanks to God. Each exclamation
is a trigger to prayer. I find myself
praying for you with a glad heart.

—PHILIPPIANS 1:3–4 MSG

I led a small group of college girls here in Nashville for almost four years. When I moved home to Nashville after doing college ministry in Edinburgh, Scotland, for six months, I knew I was moving home with hope of getting involved in the lives of college students here in town.

Cross Point Church had a service that was focused on college students at the time, and that's where I was introduced to the little crew of gals that started meeting at my house in the winter of 2012. At the beginning, in those first few weeks when we sat in a circle in my living room, I had a basket of questions that we passed around each week, and each girl had to pull a question and answer it.

What are you afraid of?

What's your favorite dessert?

Dream vacation location?

Why did you join this small group?

We covered a whole gamut of things every week just in the opening questions. We always ate dinner together—in fact, in the last four years I feel like I have really become quite competent in cooking meals for twelve. My girls eat like they are college male athletes, so I rarely have much left over. If I do, they always congregate back in the kitchen after group and grab baggies and scavenge any crumbs that might remain.

Before I became allergic to dairy and before I quit gluten, we ate a lot of casseroles. If there is one thing a Southern girl learns as she is growing up, it is how to use cream of chicken soup to combine meat and vegetables, even though I can't really tell you what cream of chicken is (and what I imagine it is grosses me out). So I've known how to make casseroles—breakfast or dinner—for the entirety of my life. It came in handy when I was trying to feed a crowd. But then once my eating changed, so did the casserole opportunities. No longer able to mix sour cream with chicken and carrots, I had to find other alternatives. No longer serving ice cream bars, I had to come up with desserts that were healthy (or healthy-ish) for the girls. As my eating changed, so did what the gals ate every Tuesday night.

It usually went pretty well, especially when I asked Pinterest to help me find a new recipe. "Feeding the 12" became the board I populated the most, loading it with big family recipes, because I thought the title was hilariously witty, and I needed help feeding all the people. I remember only one meal being a complete failure. Sure, Hannah didn't like the weeks I served fish, and April always cringed if she even SENSED there was a mushroom in the building, but the only total failure was the Crock-Pot baked potatoes. I promise I followed the rules exactly as Pinterest told me—wrapping them each in aluminum foil, stacking them in the Crock-Pot, leaving it on alllll day long. When it was time to eat, they were mostly cooked through, but they were a weird color. And each one tasted like metal, as if the aluminum foil infused the potato. I thought for sure I'd lose some girls after that meal. Gratefully, everyone came back the next Tuesday.

But in my heart I knew even bad cooking wouldn't keep them from our Tuesday nights. In their first semester as freshmen, we made a decision as a group. We were going to stick it out until they graduated. There were a few older girls in there, but the majority were the same class, so we decided that whatever we were starting here, we were going to see to the end.

I need people like that in my life. I need people who are committed to staying. It helps me commit too—to being honest, to being present, to allowing people into the corners that tend to stay dark and hidden. I'm willing to show people the corners if they plan to stay. And that's who we became for one another, every Tuesday night of the school year for four years in a row.

We had an understanding among our group—say what you need to say, ask what you need to ask, because we aren't going anywhere. When Anne and Melissa got in a fight over roommate issues, we sat on my couch together, and they both said the real stuff and survived it. When Karen got her feelings hurt by Heather and Jennifer, I made pancakes, and we all sat in my living room while maple syrup and tears poured. But they survived it. When Brandi felt attacked because no one liked her boyfriend, she was hurt, but she survived it.

A couple of girls moved away, but none of them quit. That's the thing. There were multiple arguments, hard conversations, tears were a weekly occurrence (but so was dessert), and we studied the Bible and prayed and listened to God and worshipped. We did lots of things, but we never quit.

I think of Exodus 17. Moses sends Joshua out to fight the Amalekites. As Joshua is out in the battle, if Moses's hands are raised, the Israelite army is winning. Any time he puts his hands down because his arms are tired, the Amalekites advance. So while Moses is standing at the top of the hill watching the battle below, they roll a rock over for him to sit on, and his brother Aaron and his brother-in-law Hur come and hold up his arms. They stayed by him, holding up his arms, until the sunset. All. Day. Long.

I love that visual. Having the people in your life that will hold you up when you are too tired to keep doing what you are called to do. It takes away some of the guilt I feel when I am tired to remember that Moses got tired too. Moses didn't try to do this on his own. In fact, in Exodus 18, his father-in-law reminds Moses again that he can't do this in his own strength; it is too much for one man to carry. He had to persevere—he had to keep his hands up even when he felt like he was unable to do it anymore—to ensure there was victory, but he couldn't do it alone. He needed his people.

My girls grew to need one another like that. It was beautiful to watch, painful at times, frustrating more than I probably want to admit, and many weeks, exhausting. But so beautiful. And I needed them too. I love my people, and I'm pretty eyes wide-open to the ones God brings into my life to stand beside me and hold my arms and whose arms I want to hold as well. And those girls are that for me and for one another.

I have a group text with my lifelong best friends—Haley, Molly, and Misti. Group texting is such a victory for us because we are now able to communicate pretty much constantly. Whether it is needing help with kids or recipe suggestions or real deep hurts and PLEASE PRAY NOWs, or ridiculous gifs, we are always there for each other.

When I need to say the really honest thing, when I need to spew my frustrations, I go to them. I'm not afraid to complain about being single or about missing a flight or about some family drama because I know they aren't going anywhere. They aren't scared of me or my issues. I know we are committed to one another, as best we can be for as long as we can be.

The beauty of growing up in Marietta, Georgia, but living in Nashville, Tennessee, is that it is only a three-and-a-half-hour drive. A few months ago one of them had a family emergency, and I was able to be there in just a few hours, with a strawberry cake in hand, ready to sit on the floor with the three of them and cry and eat cake until we were almost sick.

And when my broken crazy got bad, I told them. While I was still on that beach trip, lying by the pool, I texted them all and told them the truth. The next week Molly rode the Megabus all the way to Nashville just to be with me in it. Just to hold my hands up. It wasn't an intervention or a big deal; she just didn't want me to be alone.

People can be that for you.

When I first moved to Nashville, the friends I met made the move bearable.

When I first moved to Edinburgh, Scotland, the part that kept me from massive homesickness was the people that invited me into their lives.

When I travel to speak, I almost always bring a friend with me because that's what makes me feel the most normal and the most Annie.

When I traveled to Israel, I came home with a few new life-long friends.

God keeps using humans in my life to help me keep going. Whether it's the friends on the plane reminding me to fix my life when the broken crazy got so bad, or my counselor, or the friends today on Instagram reminding me that finishing this book really matters, I feel like God sets all those people on the side of the road as I am running my race.

I ran a half marathon once. I talk about it a lot because I've only done it once, and I only plan to do it once. It was 13.1 miles of chafing torture. Five of my friends also ran it, but they were in much better shape and much faster runners, so with my blessing, they left me in the dust before the first mile was even completed.

Right as I started mile twelve, over three hours into the race, I noticed someone running toward me. I was part walking / part jogging / part barely surviving, and this young woman was coming straight toward me. It took me a minute to realize it was my friend, Katie. Katie had finished the race over an hour before. But here she was, beginning at the finish line and running the course backwards until she found me.

I asked her what in the world she was doing. "I just came back to finish with you," she said with a smile. I couldn't believe it. Katie ran an extra 2.2 miles just to find me and help me finish. She encouraged me as we ran, as we finished together. She didn't let me quit; she didn't even let me walk when I wanted to walk. She just kept telling me how glad I would be when we finished.

I'll never forget that. I'll never forget that Katie sacrificed her own comfort to hold my arms up in a time of need, when I don't know that I would have gotten victory on my own.

I'm a people person. I'm always extraverted, and I barely know a stranger. But more than just a person who likes humans,

I'm particularly a MY people person. I absolutely love my friends and family. I believe you are shaped by the people you surround yourself with, and I am deeply shaped by the people around me.

I spend the most time with our little group of single girls here in Nashville. There are about ten of us, and we all speak the same language. We all believe in God and one another. We all have found careers we love and a class at the gym we love (b.fab. fitness!). We eat out too much and travel together often. The best part of a group text between ten people is if you send out a "Who wants to get BBQ for dinner?" there's a chance that at least one person will be available. Sometimes, rarely, it's all of us. But usually at least three of us decide to eat together, or see a movie, or fly to Albuquerque for a Lady Antebellum show.

These women are great for fun. But they are also great when things aren't great. We've cried together over breakups and heartache and job failures and family pain. In a world that works hard to make us feel alone in our singleness, we lock arms and refuse to hear it. We are not alone.

You need someone to remind you of that. And sometimes it feels like we have no one. Whether it's scrolling through Instagram and seeing what you are missing out on or not knowing whom to call when you need a voice on the other side, it can feel like this planet is very lonely. I get that. I feel that at times too.

When I first moved to Nashville, I had acquaintances but no friends. And in that season is when it became very real to me that Jesus could be a Friend who sticks closer than a brother (Prov. 18:24). It's not like someone sat with me at dinner, but something beautiful happened when I started asking Him to be my Friend, my close Friend. While I was still alone, and while we aren't meant to do life by ourselves, Jesus stepped in to an empty spot in my heart. And then, as I made friends and these circles of relationships grew, I was so grateful for the season when He solidified His spot as my closest Friend.

My small-group girls, my Marietta besties, my single gals in Nashville. They are the ones that hold my hands up, that come back to where I'm struggling in any kind of race and help me finish. And they are the ones I run toward as well.

It's not about the number of people you have; it's just about having even one person that can hold your arms up when things get hard. It could be your mother or your husband or your coworker. It could be your small group or softball team. It could be your best friend or your twenty best friends.

Our last small group was on a Tuesday night in April. The girls were all stressed and busy, trying to get all their senior projects turned in. I made them dinner, and I cried while I bought the groceries. When the girls arrived, an awkward heaviness hung over us. This was really it; we were ending. They loaded up their plates with grilled chicken and all piled into the living room, sliding into their usual seats on the sofas and on the floor. We talked for a bit about what was next and what we had meant to one another. This was their chance, I told them. We didn't need an emotional scene necessarily, but this was the last time we'd be like this; and if they had things to say to one another, if they wanted to express their love or gratitude, this was the time.

And they did. It was beautiful and personal and demonstrated that every bit of the time they've invested to hold one another's arms high in the air was worth it. I told them what I still believe is true. We didn't do relationship perfectly, but we did right by this group and by one another. We did that right.

We prayed, and as I said, "Amen," no one spoke. We all sat right where we were and wept those quiet tears that remind you that it all mattered.

I'll never forget that night. I'll never forget those girls, and that's not just because a group picture is framed in my living room. I won't forget them because they taught me, like Haley and Misti and Molly have, like Katie did when she ran back to help me finish, that without your people, without letting them in and letting them know you, you won't be able to persevere. Your people remind you of the goodness of God and remind you of what it means to finish.

LOOK FOR LOVELY

Who is your person? Who holds your arms up? Find them, thank them, hug them. Whose arms are you holding up?

A PICTURE IN
TEL AVIV

pray for the peace of Jerusalem.

—PSALM 122:6

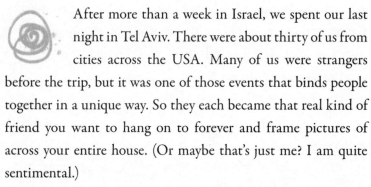

After more than a week in Israel, we spent our last night in Tel Aviv. There were about thirty of us from cities across the USA. Many of us were strangers before the trip, but it was one of those events that binds people together in a unique way. So they each became that real kind of friend you want to hang on to forever and frame pictures of across your entire house. (Or maybe that's just me? I am quite sentimental.)

We ate a late dinner at the hotel. Then a lot of us walked down to the bar that was across the street on the beach of the Mediterranean Sea. This seaside restaurant bordered off its tables with red skinny pyramid lights, about five feet in height, all lit up. We grabbed a bunch of chairs and tables, circled them up, and sat down. I walked to the edge of the sea and waded into the pitch-black water, only about two feet in, because I didn't want to get eaten by a sea animal at night, but I definitely wanted to touch the Mediterranean.

At this point, eight days in with only one to go, I was beginning to mourn the loss of this time together. The breeze was blowing, and my hair was getting sea salty. It was still warm outside, even though it was almost midnight, but I felt happy not to be sweating anymore. I listened to my guy friends talk but also tried to breathe in the moment and look around and almost memorize every detail of what was going on. The simplicity of sitting around a table on the beach with Ryan and Matthew and Ross, hearing Jessica and Jon talking over my shoulder, watching some of the other guys swimming in the ocean, seeing Grant and Kim swapping stories. I wanted to memorize it, begging my mind not to forget the red haze of the pyramid lights or the menu that was in Hebrew and English, what everyone was wearing and drinking and saying. I wanted to remember it all, and I was terrified that I wouldn't be able to.

I knew that the next night we'd all be getting on an airplane, and after flying eleven hours, we'd land in America and all go our separate ways—back to our homes, our families, our cities—and we would never be here, like this, again. And that broke my heart, even while I was still sitting around the circle with my friends. I'm weird like that. I get supersad about something ending before it ever ends. Instead of appreciating a lightning bug when it is illuminating the night, I watch it and get sad about when it will go away. Maybe this is why, as a kid, I always collected lightning bugs in mason jars. I wanted to collect and hold all those bright moments and never let them go. But sometimes they go, they leave, they stop. I started to feel panic, sitting on that beach, like I was watching the lightning bugs lose their twinkle as the minutes ticked away.

I thought about how I almost didn't go on this trip. To be honest, I've always been a little afraid to go to Israel. Fear isn't often a guiding emotion for me, but when I listened to the news and read online about Israel, it always seemed to be getting bombed.

I try not to go places that are getting bombed.

So in 2014 when Josh from the Israel Collective reached out to me, first via e-mail and then in a phone call, and offered for me to join a team that was going to Israel, I thought it sounded cool, but I mainly thought it sounded dangerous, so I said no thanks.

Six months later I changed my mind, and in September 2015, I went to Israel with thirty people I did not know.

But it only took eight days to feel like they were my people and like some part of me never wanted this trip to end. (And, just a note, I felt absolutely safe the entire time.) I'm a physical touch person; and in situations like this, sitting on the beach in Tel Aviv, when my foot kicked Matthew because he made a dumb joke or I high-fived Ross because I absolutely agree that doughnuts are a food group, I started to mourn because I knew this was what I was going to lose when we all returned home. We could FaceTime and phone chat and text every waking hour, but physical presence would be gone.

As the night wore on, conversations continued, and people began to head slowly back to the hotel, one or two at a time. I was also running out of steam. I was so tired, and we still had another full day ahead of us before we were scheduled to fly out, but I didn't want to miss one minute with my friends. My eyelids were drooping; the guys were all still wide-awake. So I knew I had to go to bed, but I was just so sad about it. Because it was the end.

When you collect the moments that matter, it means the moments have passed. And that's sometimes hard for me. I see the value in them, clearly, and the importance of remembering what it felt like to slide my feet in that sand and listen to the guys talk about theology and tacos and Texas; and recalling that memory, even today, strengthens me.

Why do I still feel sad today, at home in Nashville, and yet smile when I think of that night on the beach? How can that be? How can sadness and joy coexist? How can a memory that makes me so happy also be a memory that brings sadness?

Paul was so faithful in his letters from prison to remind the churches, always in the first few sentences, of how he was thanking God for them and their partnership in spreading the gospel.

Paul was pulling strength from these memories of friends and stories he continued to hear, even though he wasn't with them, even while imprisoned.

As you know, I'm a pain avoider, and yet I have a bad habit of tossing out the memories I need because they also hurt. But I've realized there is something beautiful, and something that opens your heart in new and deeper ways, when you open yourself up to experience pain as well as joy. I think that has to be part of all of this. Maybe that's what it means to rejoice in our sufferings as Paul says in Romans 5? Maybe when we make our hearts available to the hard moments and allow ourselves to experience God's love in new ways, we are also increasing our capacity to love others.

I feel that with these new friends. At the end of a two-year journey toward mental and physical and spiritual health, here are these guys who are meeting Post-Broken Crazy Annie. I am more open and braver and kinder because I remember the pain of the broken crazy, and I remember all the things that led to the breakdown, and while I don't relish any new pain, I don't put it in a box and shove it into the back corner of my heart, either. There is a chance I love them more because of what has transpired over the last few years. And that's not about them; that's about me.

Ryan and Ross and Matthew walked me back to the hotel because it was getting late and I didn't want to star in any television show about an author being abducted in Tel Aviv. So, they were my bodyguards. We called the elevator; and while waiting, we turned around toward the mirrored wall and took a picture. I have the picture hanging above my desk, and I see it every day as I write: my hair is plastered to my head, and my jeans are rolled up and soaked to the knee. Matthew's hat is pushed back; he's wearing a black compression sleeve under his white T-shirt because of a pretrip injury, Ryan and Ross are both holding their tennis shoes in their hands, and Ryan has a beach towel thrown over his shoulder. Matthew is taking the picture, so we're all turned toward him. Our faces all say the same thing with different looks, but we are all expressing something about how we feel just standing there with one another.

When the elevator arrived that night in Tel Aviv, I said good night and took the elevator to the fourth floor. I walked into my room, and before the door was even closed behind me, I was crying. I cried because I was scared. I was scared that when this trip was over, the friendships were going to end as well. I've been to enough summer camps to know what happens when you are there and when you are home, and I didn't want it to happen, the slow fade of communication. I was scared I was going to lose them when we got home, and I was scared of that loss, and I was scared I wouldn't know what to do with my fear. It all felt new to me, maybe because parts of my heart are new, so I was feeling the new parts of my heart break. It was my lightning bug fear manifesting in friendships I didn't want to blink out.

I was scared that collecting these moments would feel like trying to hold onto bubbles or wind or ice cream. I was scared the tighter I tried to grip the more I'd panic, and these moments would slip through my fingers; and while I'm freaking out about losing them, they would be gone.

I said as much to the Lord that night in Tel Aviv. I started with thanks because I couldn't believe He let us all travel together and kept us safe, but then I told Him I was worried and scared. I told Him I didn't know how to collect memories I wish weren't stories with endings. I asked Him how to do this, how to navigate these new healthy heart moments that felt so deeply sad.

And I felt like He asked me to trust Him. To let Him hold the things my hands cannot grasp. While I collect moments, He will collect friendships and make them last.

I think that may be the trick to this whole looking for lovely business. I think confessing to God when it seems hard or scary or painful, confessing what you want to do but what feels too challenging—it's what helps you finish. It's what helps you see Him in the people you meet and in the moments when you have to let them leave.

So I decided to believe God, that He is who holds all things together, including that squad, those memories, my heart. My phone beeped that night in my hotel room as Matthew texted over that picture; and as I stared at it, I knew that for months and years to come, this one simple photograph would be my lightning bug that would never go out.

LOOK FOR LOVELY

Pull out an old photo album and look at the people. What did they mean to you? How did they matter? Which folks could you reach out to today and tell them what they mean to you?

GARDENS

He has made everything beautiful in its time. He has also set eternity in the human heart; yet no one can fathom what God has done from beginning to end.

—ECCLESIASTES 3:11 NIV

I laced up my mint-and-gray tennis shoes and threw on my raincoat. It had rained all day in New York City, and by 1:00 p.m., it was barely slowing down. I had been sitting at the desk in this tiny apartment, rented on Airbnb, for the entire morning, writing. It was time to let my legs do some work while my fingers and brain rested. I didn't have a real destination, except I wanted a smoothie from a lime-green storefront on East 9th Street and 1st Avenue. I walked toward Tompkins Square Park, mainly because Mumford and Sons wrote an entire song about it, so I tried to go past it at least once a day during my stay. I kept walking, Hillsong United in my earbuds, until I realized I was almost to the East River. Oops.

IN SEARCH OF LOVELY

Time to turn around. At Avenue C, headed back west, I made a left-hand turn off of 10th and decided to go ahead and hop on 9th to go up toward the smoothie.

Looking down at my phone to answer a text message, I crossed over Avenue C and started walking up 9th Avenue. To my left, a garden. I put my phone back in the raincoat pocket and slowed my pace to look more closely. Huge weeping willow trees flung their branches over the fence and onto the sidewalk, creating a little protection from the rain. I could look through the fence to see a beautiful and well-kept garden, full of plants and benches and stone paths. And though I couldn't quite see the fullness of it, was that an amphitheater back there? I think it was.

Across the top of the chain-link fence were these multicolored flowers of all sizes and shades, made from old cans and bottles. The cans had been cut into strips, from top to bottom, while still being attached to the base. Then the strips were curled outward, like petals on a flower. Some different-colored bottle caps and such were used for the center of the flowers. It was just old trash, treasured, folded around, and turned into something beautiful. And there were so many of them, all tightly bundled together like bouquets or fields or those cases of flowers in grocery stores. It stretched for half the block or so.

I lingered at the garden's fence, watching the lone rooster that was just on the other side of the locked gate, studying each unique handmade flower attached to the fence just above my head out of reach. I pulled my phone out and started taking piles of pictures. I read the sign on the gate: La Plaza Cultural.[8] And I felt like I had found my garden, the one that understood me, the one that took trash and made it into a treasure.

I thought the bus ride was going to be longer. We stood on top of the Mount of Olives and took a group picture overlooking the city of Jerusalem, and Joav, our tour guide, taught us about the ancient city of David. A man with a camel kept trying to get us to ride it, and another guy with silver necklaces wove in and out of our group trying to sell his goods.

We finished up at the overlook and got back on the bus, immediately looking for our "bus buddies." It was a system set up on day one of the trip—everyone pick a person and each time we get on the bus, make sure your buddy is on there, too. Most people, upon entering the bus and finding their seat, just did hand signals or looked around, but for me and my bus buddy, it was different. Every time we were told to check, I hollered, "BYRON!" and Byron yelled, "ANNIE!" and it probably made the rest of our team crazy, but Byron didn't get left in Israel at any point, and neither did I. So. Success.

We started to drive, and just a few minutes later the driver pulled over again, and we all hopped out, headed to the garden of Gethsemane. *Right here?* I thought, *But we're right by the city of Jerusalem?*

I think in my mind, *The garden where Jesus prayed and suffered before being arrested was far out of town.* I pictured this secluded garden, miles from the action. And yet here we were, literally yards from the walls of Jerusalem, in this little patch of nature.

Joav spoke to us for a few minutes, reminding us what historians believe happened right where we were standing. And then he gave us some time to walk around the garden and think and pray.

I walked around for a few minutes, then eventually stopped and stood on the western side of the garden. It's blocked off by metal fencing and a half wall made of cement and bricks. I leaned up against the bricks and set my Bible on the cement ledge, just at the height of my hips. I turned to Matthew 26, the story that happened right in this very garden.

> *Then Jesus went with his disciples to a place called Gethsemane, and he said to them, "Sit here while I go over there and pray." He took Peter and the two sons of Zebedee along with him, and he began to be sorrowful and troubled. Then he said to them, "My soul is overwhelmed with sorrow to the point of death. Stay here and keep watch with me."*

Going a little farther, he fell with his face to the ground and prayed, "My Father, if it is possible, may this cup be taken from me. Yet not as I will, but as you will."

Then he returned to his disciples and found them sleeping. "Couldn't you men keep watch with me for one hour?" he asked Peter. "Watch and pray so that you will not fall into temptation. The spirit is willing, but the flesh is weak."

He went away a second time and prayed, "My Father, if it is not possible for this cup to be taken away unless I drink it, may your will be done."

When he came back, he again found them sleeping, because their eyes were heavy. So he left them and went away once more and prayed the third time, saying the same thing.

Then he returned to the disciples and said to them, "Are you still sleeping and resting? Look, the hour has come, and the Son of Man is delivered into the hands of sinners. Rise! Let us go! Here comes my betrayer!" (Matt. 26:36–46 NIV)

These verses, in my Bible, spread over two pages. The first paragraph sits on the bottom of the left page, and the rest is the top of the right page. I read these verses over and over again as the tears puddled in my eyes. I stopped reading and just started to rub my hands over the words and talk to Jesus. It was here, I just kept thinking, in this spot where He decided I was worth the sacrifice. It was here that He made the actual decision—I am saved right now because He was willing right here. If I can't hug Him and thank Him face-to-face, I will rub the pages where His name and suffering sit and pray my guts out in thankfulness.

The tears wouldn't stop. I'm such an emoter that I kept telling myself to dry it up and calm down, but after two or three minutes, I gave in to it. I decided to let my heart break. I had felt this before. Heartbreak has happened a time or two in my life, but this was different.

I felt His kindness.

And His kindness toward me in this place, in my sin, needing salvation, broke my heart.

I stood there crying for a lot of minutes. I just let the tears fall as long as they needed to, knowing I may never stand in that spot again. My soul, my insides, my guts needed to say all the things my mouth didn't know how to say. So I cried, I ran my fingers over the words of this story over and over again, and I whispered, "Thank You, thank You, thank You."

I turned and faced Jerusalem. There it was, just across the street. And my mind blinked back to that garden on 9th and Avenue C in New York City. And I understood Jesus better in that second than I ever had.

He was a city guy who loved a little piece of nature. Just like me and my walk around the East Village. He went looking for lovely in Jerusalem and ended up, repeatedly the Scriptures tell us, at the garden of Gethsemane. In fact, Luke 22:39 says that

Jesus went out "as usual" to the Mount of Olives, where the garden is located. Looking at Jerusalem's wall, just over there from where I stood, I saw a side of Jesus I had never seen—the part of Him that sought out beauty, just as I do. The part of Him that found rest in nature, that part of Him that may have also been drawn to La Plaza Cultural and the long branches of the weeping willow. I'm like that too. The part of Him that loved the city but just needed some alone time, time away, outside of the city, to pray and remember why He loved the city in the first place.

What is it about gardens that draws us in, people like you and me and Jesus? Particularly, what is it about tiny grassy knolls in the center of town or community-grown plots of land or moments of nature just outside the hustle of the city?

I've found my garden in Nashville, too. And it has absolutely changed my life.

LOOK FOR LOVELY

Take a walk today. Maybe it's just around the block, or maybe go to the local mall and take a few laps. While you are walking, look around. What do you see? What is catching your eye? Pray as you walk, asking God to direct your eyes to the things He doesn't want you to miss.

WHEN YOU FIND LOVELY

I have two stress fractures in my right foot. I don't really know when the incident happened that brought them about, but alas, they are here. I'm prone to injury, which is why I pay for health insurance. It's not that I'm all that clumsy—well, maybe I am—but I do get hurt a lot. Knock on wood, my immune system is pretty strong after spending five years teaching in the public school system, so I don't often get sick. But injuries? I catch them all the time. Or drop them on my foot or trip over them.

After being in pain for a few weeks, I finally went to the doctor. And as he pushed on the swollen spot outside of my foot, like squeezing a trigger on a water gun, the tears rushed out. He patted my knee, told me we had some fractures, and gave me a plastic boot. (Well, I bought a plastic boot, but the bill didn't come for a week or so, so I walked out with it like it was a gift.) It has really messed up my mojo and taken away one of the things I love most: time at Radnor Lake.

It was the week of my thirty-fourth birthday, and my family was in town to celebrate. My parents had recently gotten on a hiking kick, so they asked if there was somewhere around my house where we could hike. I called my old roommate Laura. She had told me how she meets friends to hike sometimes, and so I thought she would be the one to help me out with a local hiking spot.

"Radnor Lake," her text read. "It is the best." And then she gave me directions on how to get there and where to park and what trails to do with my family. And we followed her directions completely. It was a beautiful walk, not too difficult but good exercise. We saw tiny baby deer and mama deer. We saw a couple of turkeys—WILD TURKEYS!—and we were merely ten minutes outside of the big city.

It was beautiful and fun, and I absolutely loved it.

I've long found nature to be a place where I connect with God. The mountains at sunrise. The beach at sunset. It can all leave me speechless with its beauty. But for some reason I had never connected hiking with beauty—probably because I considered it exercise; and as you know, exercise, traditionally, was no fun for me.

But, surprising even myself, I had such a good time walking the trails with my family that I decided to go back the next week. Just me.

I parked and walked up to the map of the trails right at the entrance of the lake trail, and because I so fear getting lost (it's a skill I have, leaving a place and never knowing how to get back from whence I came), I took lots of pictures of the map. I wanted to walk the same path my family and I had done the week before. My body was unhealthy and didn't want to exercise, but I had sniffed out what felt like something lovely with my family, and it was worth circling around again to see if I was right.

The fishermen in Jesus' time worked like this, eyes wide open to little glimmers of hope. In fact, when we meet Peter, he is doing this one particular type of fishing using an amphiblestron net. (I mean, no WAY did they call it that, right? Such a hard word. But that's the modern translation for us English speakers.) This kind of net is used in the shallower water and held in the hands of the fisherman. The edges of the nets are weighted so that when the net is thrown in the water, it will sink to the bottom, catching everything in that area. The fisherman then tightens the string he never threw out, and it collects together the edges of the net, closing it in on the fish in the middle.

Peter didn't just throw the net haphazardly, tossing it out and bringing it in over and over all day long. He would stand still and quiet in the more shallow parts of the Sea of Galilee, with it's rocky and muddy bottom, and watch intently. When he saw a shimmering fish swim by, he knew there were probably more around. So that would be the cue to throw the net, hoping that by seeing one fish and trying to catch it, he would run into an entire school.

That's how I felt going back to Radnor. I had seen one little shimmering hope of joy found in exercise, and so I wanted to throw out my net and see if there was more to be caught there.

I started going once a week or so, listening to preaching podcasts on my walk every day. I would find one about forty-five minutes long; and if I pressed play right when I began on the wood chip-covered path, I would finish by the time I made the loop and got back to my car. It wasn't long before I was wanting to go twice a week, just to be outside. And I started to see that my heart loved being at Radnor Lake, but so did my body. It was just a matter of weeks before I was finishing that trail quicker than the forty-five-minute podcasts. I would sit in my silver Toyota Camry and listen to the last few minutes of the podcast, wondering what in the world happened different this particular time that made it so there were minutes left on the podcast.

(Um, Annie? You're getting stronger and faster. Yahoo.)

The map had shown me there were "medium" and "difficult" trails all around Radnor Lake, and so far I was just doing "easy." So on a Wednesday in the fall, I decided to try the "medium" trail.

I cannot put into words what a big deal this was for me (clearly, I'm going to try). For a quitter, for someone who traditionally has hated exercise and found no beauty in it at all, I was surprised at myself. Whatever I caught that first time walking at Radnor gave me the strength to want to do more, to throw out my net again, to challenge myself more, and to walk farther.

Because I had never thought about it, and because I had never really made the choice to persevere when things got hard, I had never experienced this emotion—the feelings of someone who finished one thing that was hard, so they pushed themselves to something even more difficult. (To be fair to myself, I've probably done that in some arenas before but certainly not in personal exercise or how I treated my body.)

The first day on the medium trail was *so* hard. The hills were serious, and the path was long. I looked at a map before heading out—even took a new picture of it with my phone, just focusing on this particular "medium" path. My earbuds in, I walked on the dirt path for ten to fifteen minutes, thinking, praying, processing. Two particular situations were in my mind—the first an invitation I had received to speak at an event, and the second had to do with a single man in my life. Neither had a clear right and wrong answer to me. Both were opportunities, options, chances that may be worth taking. I rolled them around in my head like marbles bouncing with each step I took.

I was worried, though. I was worried that I was going to miss what God had for me because I couldn't see the RIGHT or WRONG of the situations. "Just show me, Lord," I was saying, "and I'll do what You want. I just don't know where either of these is going."

I suddenly looked down and realized I did not know where I was, and I was pretty sure I was going the wrong way. Since I had never been here, I didn't know if I had possibly (GOD FORBID) hopped onto the "difficult" trail, or if I had somehow made a wrong turn. Everywhere I looked was brown path and green trees and dark shadows. Frustration crept up my back and pushed on my shoulders as I realized I was feeling that kind of confusion in lots of areas of my life—particularly those two situations that I couldn't get out of my brain and here, on this path. A little lost, a little sure I was wrong, a little concerned that I was missing the right thing.

I also thought I may be lost in these woods.

When in a blink, God stamped a statement onto my heart. TRUST THE PATH.[9]

I looked down at my feet, at the path, and I realized what I knew was true—the path would take me back to the road eventually. I had seen it on the map, I knew I wasn't the first to do it, and the way the path was created, it ended at the road, a few hundred yards from the parking lot.

TRUST THE PATH, I heard God say. And I knew He didn't just mean the "medium" difficulty one at Radnor Lake.

He meant the questions in my heart, the things I wonder about, the worries that I am going to miss Him. I don't have to know where things are going; I don't have to know the destination; I just have to trust the path.

Maybe Peter had similar moments throughout his journey when he had to go back to what he knew, the moment Jesus said the words, "Follow Me." He didn't know what was coming next; he just had to trust that those sandals on the path in front of him were leading to a good place. So while there were moments in his life following Christ that were hard for Peter, he could go back to this moment and trust the One who is sovereign over the path before him.

God has repeatedly shown up for me like this at Radnor Lake. It feels like our place now. It's not just the beauty of the changing leaves; it's what He whispers to me around every corner. It's the joy I felt from Him when the medium path got too easy and I decided, after a year of walking, that the difficult path might be worth a try. It doesn't feel like God cares about my changing body or my strengthening leg muscles as much as He cares that my heart has gotten stronger and my resolve has changed.

Radnor Lake helped me quit quitting.

I've long wanted a second tattoo. It's exactly as they say—the big hard decision is between zero tattoos and one; the less hard decision is adding to your collection. While "grace" graced my left wrist, my right wrist was barren, waiting patiently for the next word I felt would define me.

One day, walking the medium path at Radnor, I listened to a sermon about the secrets of a Spirit-filled life. As I huffed and puffed up the hills and around the curves of the trail, I agreed with all the preacher was saying and thought, *Yeah, I've got this stuff. I'm working it out.*

And then the last secret he said is, "Christians today need perseverance."

I stopped. My spirit immediately felt a catch. I lacked perseverance. I knew it. I knew I was broken, I knew the broken crazy had a purpose, and I realized this was it. I was learning to persevere, as I was learning to look for lovely. The longer I looked for lovely, the more I kept going, the less I quit. But I had to keep choosing to persevere. Just as it says in Romans 5, I could already see that in my little bit of walking the trails, the suffering has made me persevere, my character (and strength) had grown, and I had hope to keep going. God was showing me in nature, and in my body, what has always been true in my spirit if I would choose to see it that way. He was literally changing me from the inside out.

I listened through that particular podcast sermon every day at Radnor for the next week.

And I knew what word I wanted on my right wrist.

Persevere.

I went to dinner with Connor and Keenan, two of my Vandybros, and I had seen perseverance in them. It's one of those athlete things. They knew what it meant to never give up. So while we waited for our Mexican dinner to arrive at the table, I brought out a piece of paper and a pen and had them each write the word over and over again. Just like Molly and *grace*, I wanted this tattoo to be in the handwriting of people who live it already. I wanted their spirit of perseverance to be branded on my arm.

Right before Christmas Connor and Jared, another Vandybro, went with me to the tattoo parlor and watched as my skinny little wrist got branded in white ink with Connor's handwriting. *Persevere.*

It makes perfect sense to me, grace and perseverance. I have learned that to be all grace is to be lazy but to be all perseverance is to be judgmental. A good balance of grace and perseverance pushes us forward without destroying our spirit when we don't meet a goal, and it continually brings us back to our goals, dreams, and desires in order to remember why we began, how far we have come to get here, and where we ultimately want to go. It gives us permission to not be perfect but to strive toward excellence. Just like when my hands are clasped together, I want my life to be marked by grace and perseverance as partners.

My tattoo says *persevere*. Because I'm not trying to remember the concept of perseverance, I'm bossing myself around. PERSEVERE, DOWNS, I hear when I look down at it. When I am on that difficult trail and I'm teary because it is hard, I want to look down at my wrist and see the directive, from God to the pastor's mouth to Connor's hand to me. "Persevere, Annie," I say to myself. "Keep going." I rub my left hand across the tattoo, like my thumbs across the pages of the book of Matthew at the garden of Gethsemane, because I want to feel the word and remember what it means to me.

I think Jesus would love Radnor Lake and the trails because it reminds me of His garden. Just outside of town, nature at it's best, a place where the connection to God is clear and constant.

And you should hear me as I get to my car every day now. I try to jog the last few minutes on the paved path heading back toward the parking lot, and as soon as my hand can touch any part of my car, I say out loud: "I didn't quit. I'm not a quitter. I'm a finisher."

Because that's never been true of me like it is now. I'm a finisher. I don't quit.

What has happened to me at Radnor Lake, each day's walk building something in my soul, has affected every area of my life. God has used that place as the incubator for my growth and change. My hunch that throwing out my amphiblestron net would catch me something beautiful was right, and it ended up filling my net to capacity and overflowing.

-*Section 3*-

WHEN I FOUND LOVELY

PERSPECTIVE
SHIFTS

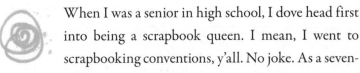When I was a senior in high school, I dove head first into being a scrapbook queen. I mean, I went to scrapbooking conventions, y'all. No joke. As a seventeen-year-old. (I was a funny kid.) But I wanted so badly to have a beautiful piece of art at the end of my senior year that would become an heirloom for myself and my family. I used my babysitting money to buy all the best products, like stickers and paper and interestingly shaped scissors and a CORNER ROUNDER because I was big-time.

My mother has some photo albums from her high school and college days, and I would pore over them as a kid, trying to see the life of this adult woman that lived in my house with me, but to see her like me, as a teenager. I wanted to see her life before I existed. I loved it. I was fascinated to stare at her friends, to read what people wrote to her in her yearbooks, to see the pieces of art she made for my grandparents. I loved getting to know her before she knew me. And as I entered into my senior year, I wanted to make a scrapbook like that for my kids someday. (Or, as the case may be, for me to go back and look almost twenty years later and laugh at many of my decisions, particularly when it came to how often I wore a ponytail. Dear Annie, WEAR YOUR HAIR DOWN SOMETIMES. Sheesh.)

Mom collected memories from her high school and college life. So the propensity to collect things is a little bit in me already. My grandfather, who recently passed away just a week shy of his 102nd birthday, was an absolute hoarder, so I know it's in my blood going back at least two generations.

That skill has actually turned out to be handy for me. But in the last two years, since the broken crazy, God has opened my eyes to all these little moments of lovely around me, the ones we've talked about here and so many more. Speaking at my home church's summer camp, dancing after dinner on the Sea of Galilee, praying on stage before the Q Conference in Boston.

It's not that my life is all that different; it's just that I see it differently. So it feels like a brand-new life. I know, I know. Dramatic pause and dramatic language, but I'm telling you, that is how I feel. I feel like since I gave honest words to the broken crazy and started to get healthy around it, God has shown up and walked me into more healing than I even knew to ask for. And in it He is opening my eyes.

And as I'm collecting these moments that matter, I'm actually just seeing more of Him. Because in the end that's what this is all about. When you find Jesus, you have found lovely. He is everything we need.

In the hallway of my house, that doubles as a storage unit, sits a Tupperware container of every journal I've ever written in. Upon my death, hopefully many years from now, those journals are to be burned, not read. My small group girls know this; all my friends know this. But for me this box of journals is an amazing collection of moments.

I pulled out the journal from while I was writing *Let's All Be Brave*, right as the broken crazy got real, and it's an absolute mess with barely any words. But it's a collection, for me, of moments I need never to forget. Yes, I'm a different woman now, but I respect that woman who was suffering and how she didn't give up as much as she could have.

I decided I wanted an actual jar, just as a little reminder of some moments that I want to put all in the same place, particularly the ones I have written about here. I printed out that picture from Tel Aviv and slid it down the side of the jar, with my friends' faces outward. I snatched a blue paint chip and a yellow one from the local hardware store and I dropped them in there, thanking God again for Nicole. I took an older bottle of nail polish that I wasn't going to use anymore and let it settle to the bottom of the jar. I asked my counselor for her card at an appointment recently. She looked at me quizzically, but I told her I wanted it for my jar. So it's in there too. Connor gave me a baseball from a game I attended, so that sits on the bottom, rolled right to the middle. My friend who lost his wife in the accident? Her visitation pamphlet is in there, since her loss really was a catalyst for me understanding that sometimes the only beauty in anything, especially tragedy, is that Jesus is still on the throne. I grabbed a few fallen leaves today as I walked the trails at Radnor Lake to add to the jar as well.

This journey itself, this book itself, in some crazy way, is a collection of what God has shown to be lovely. When I found lovely, both in me and in the world, it changed everything.

UNFINISHED

I've lived in the same house in Nashville for the last four years. It's a rental, it's a fixer-upper, it's a mess. The basement floods when it rains, and the doors swell in the summers. But it's way cute and homey on the inside. It has plenty of space for living, and my small-group girls have always loved it. It's a really sweet and wonderful home.

In the front yard is a lamppost that looks just like the one from *The Lion, the Witch, and the Wardrobe*. It's alongside the driveway right in front of the house, but it's most often hidden by a massively overgrown bush that looks like a tree and also has a pretty solid helping of vines weaving around it.

The lamp stands just behind that mass of green, but "stands" is a bit of a generous descriptor. It leans. Depending on the season, the lamp can be leaning just a bit, or it can be almost touching the ground, like it did last winter when it snowed. It looked like the lamp bowed down under the power of the powder. There is a lightbulb in the lamp, but it doesn't work. And the lamp has six glass panes around it, but one is dangling off, and one is missing all together.

This is the reason my home is appropriately named Broke Lamp Manor. Because if you are looking for me, you'll find me at the house with the janky lamppost in the front yard.

If I'm honest, Broke Lamp Manor is a great name for my house because it is kind of who I am, too. As much as I wish I could hide it, and as much as the rest of the house that is me can be cleaned up and a cute little place, you can't even get in the driveway without seeing the brokenness.

That's hard for me. I am one who would rather hide my brokenness, hide the lamp that is less than sufficient. But just like with my house, I feel God pushing me a bit to embrace my broken places and appreciate my weaknesses as much as I appreciate my strengths.

On the first day of fall, I flew to Oklahoma City. My friends John and Kari Sowers live there and were hosting a mentoring conference I wanted to attend. John runs The Mentoring Project, along with Donald Miller, and they truly are the experts in how to have healthy mentoring relationships. I wanted to sit in an audience full of people who love investing in the next generation, and I was stoked to listen to the professionals teach me how to better love others. During the first day I heard amazing speakers like Carey Casey, Dr. John Perkins, Rosanna Tomiuk, John Luke Robertson, Captain Wayland Cubit, and the list goes

WHEN I FOUND LOVELY

on and on. After the main-day sessions ended, a handful of us walked over to the Sowers's house for dinner.

My friends Lindsey, Matthew, and I zigzagged four blocks or so in the cool of the late afternoon until we arrived at the Sowers, tables set outside and all the doors flung open. The dining room had been transformed into a buffet of sorts and tables and chairs were lined up all the way down the driveway.

Our friends mingled through the rooms like the breeze that blew through the house, and we drank sweet tea and lemonade until it was time to eat. We loaded our plates with burgers and salad and homemade potato chips.

I have a real special spot in my heart for homemade potato chips. I find them to be heavenly when made just a little thicker, majorly crispy on the outside but just the thinnest sheet of soft potato in the middle. The Sowers offered that exact kind, so I was thrilled.

I sat down at a table outside, and as I got a few bites into my burger, John popped outside. "Let's talk about your book," he said. "I hear you're having problems." He was right. So we walked back inside, and I sat on the piano bench while he pulled up a chair, and as he ate his burger, I told him the problem. "Something is missing," I said. "I'm stuck."

And he listened as I told him my hopes and dreams and plans and where I was exactly, feeling lodged between a rock and a hard place in the writing and like logs on a dam blocking a creek, the flow of words had gotten lodged as well. John looked me right in the eyes, his Boston Red Sox hat pushed back just a bit so his face was in full view, and he said, "You know that just to finish the book doesn't require you to be a finished product, right?"

But I didn't. I didn't remember that it's okay with you, and it should be okay with me, if I'm unfinished. I stood in front of the mirror today in a hotel and was totally mean with my words and my glare to every corner of my body. I ate a Butterfinger candy bar a few nights ago because I was scared, not hungry. I haven't exercised this week, and I haven't read my Bible like I want to. Because I have been traveling so much this month, I feel disconnected from my people, and overall I just kind of feel like a mess. Not quite broken crazy level, but it feels just around the bend.

Maybe it's my own weaknesses being given voice and space, or maybe I'm really tired, and so my resolve isn't the boss I want it to be. Or maybe this is a spiritual thing, and I'm being bothered by the enemy of our souls. Either way, I'm not winning, and I'm not finished, and I want to be finished.

I want to be all right so that you will think I'm all right. I want to be victorious constantly so that you won't think I'm a failure. I want to say I find beauty around every corner, but the truth is my eye is drawn to trash as much as it is drawn to treasure.

I think often of Philippians 2:12 where it tells us to "work out" our salvation. And when I'm sitting across the table from one of my younger friends, Connor or Liz or April, for example, and we are talking about their faith questions or some struggle, I'm quick to remind them that no one is asking them to be done, no one expects perfection, and they shouldn't either. It's enough if they will just not to give up and keep working out what God is doing on the inside. Trust the process, my counselor would say.

But then when I'm looking in the mirror, or sitting down to my computer to tell you how to persevere, I feel shame that I can't invite you to a party I'm already attending. It's okay for you to be working out your salvation; it's okay for you to walk away, as Tim Shaw told me; but that doesn't mean you are quitting. But if I'm honest with myself, and you, and John Sowers, I'm not okay being unfinished.

John kept pushing me on this. Just to say out loud, on this page, that I am trying, and will be trying every day for the rest of my life, to look for lovely in the simplest places and the grandest moments. But I'm not always succeeding. I'm that guy on the football team who rarely catches a pass, but the team likes him because he still shows up for practice every day.

Everyone's mentor Bob Goff reminded me once to be the same person on the surface that I am at the depths of me. My aunt and uncle lived on a lake that used to be a town in a valley. When they decided to dam off the river and fill the valley with water to create a man-made lake for energy production, all the people moved out of the town, but they didn't destroy the buildings.

It's so freaky. You can boat all summer long, and ski and such, and never have a problem, never experience anything except a fun day on the lake. But you have to be careful in the winter, when the water is down, because just twenty to thirty feet below the surface are the roofs of homes, and in the dead of winter, you can see the steeple of the church poking out of the center of the body of water. It's a dishonest lake, actually. It wants you to believe the water is pure and clean when actually there are algae-covered buildings just thirty feet below you.

As Bob and I talked about water and depth and what lies beneath, he said, "Annie, to be authentically you, you have to be the same at one foot of depth as you are at thirty."

At one foot? I'm finished. I'm shiny. I'm clean. I'm a great Annie.

At thirty feet? I'm most definitely unfinished.

There's not much lovely about that view, but it does feel freeing to say it. And freedom is incredibly beautiful.

I guess what my friend John knows, that I needed to remember, is that for this to matter to you and feel honest to me, I have to tell you what lies below the surface today. And so here is the thirty-feet-deep view that I'm going to work to show at one foot, too:

I'm a different Annie than I used to be. I had to be broken to be rebuilt, but breakdowns seem to often come before breakthroughs, right? My cape of shame has long been trashed, and my days of constant self-hate have passed. What God has done in my heart and life (and body, to be honest) in the last two years is nothing short of a miracle. I used to be a quitter; now I cross more finish lines than I ever have before. I didn't know what it felt like for my character to be stretched and grown, but I do now. I thought I understood hope, but the kind of hope that has become mine in recent months is a treasure I don't want to release. I have surrounded myself with people who are for me, for my health, and for my sanity, and it has made for a tribe I am deeply grateful for and indebted to. I am growing and changing, and I like me more than I ever have.

And I am very unfinished. (I bet you are, too.)

But I am very loved. (I know you are, too.)

EPILOGUE

(I know. I'm not near fancy enough for an epilogue. It is something serious literary types do. I'm just Annie. But I had one more thing to say and when you have one more thing to say? You epilogue.)

THIS IS MY SONG

Even though I've got these two stress fractures in my right foot, I couldn't resist going to Radnor Lake to walk the trails. It was the first day of fall—not officially, just according to the cool weather—and so I just couldn't pass up the opportunity for the bright afternoon sun to warm me as that autumn breeze blows through the leaves and onto my skin as I walked around the lake.

A sermon was waiting for me in my podcast app, and some friends told me it was a real doozie, a good one, so I was excited about that as well. I hadn't been on the trails in about a week, which for me in the last year is a long time, especially when the weather is gorgeous.

I'm walking slower than usual, giving myself permission to let up the normal speed since I have an actual injured foot. I also take the flat path, that first path I ever walked, around toward my favorite #10 bench, as the pastor is teaching in my ears about 2 Chronicles 20 and the increase we all need of God's presence and God's victory.

I start to think about all the ways I've been looking for lovely. I think about how I'm watching for a miracle. And the pastor, as he's teaching, talks about 2 Chronicles 20:22.

> *As they began to sing and praise, the LORD set ambushes against the men of Ammon and Moab and Mount Seir who were invading Judah, and they were defeated.* (2 Chron. 20:22 NIV)

He says, "You see, when the word of the Lord does its full work in you and in me, there is a natural, normal response to God in song."

I'm not a great singer, but I resonated with what he was preaching. In fact, I almost felt like I could explode with YES and AMEN. God has done such a full and life-changing work in me in the last two years, everything you've read so far here, that I feel like a song could burst out of me at any point. I'm walking faster, I notice mainly because my foot begins to throb, and I turned the corner and dipped down that hill right by the little wooden bridge. The ground is soft because it rained yesterday, but it's not muddy; it just gives a little under my steps.

As I'm listening, I tell God I want to sing Him a song—I want a song that speaks to this season, to the healing He has done in me, to the work I know He has completed in my heart.

What is the song I want to sing to Him? And there on the path, I start to think of you, and I start to think of what I would sing to you about Jesus if that wasn't a terrible idea for your ears. And here's what came to my mind:

I would sing that He is a miracle worker, even when you aren't seeing it. I'd sing that His love is unmatched, and you can see that best in the darkness. I'd sing that my life is only because of Jesus and only for Jesus and the mess of an Annie I would be without Him is almost too painful for me to imagine. I'd sing over and over again that He knows me better than I know myself, and for all the hard days and all the confusing moments and all the pain I have faced, I wouldn't trade a minute of it because of how I know Him now. I'd share a verse about how He can be trusted, how God is your Father and Jesus is your best Friend and the Holy Spirit is here to comfort you.

I would sing that I know no greater joy than living life with Jesus, and I lack absolutely nothing because I have Him.

I'd cry when I sing it, like I cried when I thought it on the path around Radnor Lake, like I'm crying as I write. Because it's all been for this. It's all been because I want to know Jesus and I want you to know Jesus.

And as I continue to walk, in my headphones, Pastor Bill mentions something about waking up singing a song. "Pay attention," he says. "God may be giving you the song for that next season."

And I freeze. Right there across the bridge as the path pushes up a slight incline, I stop trying to write the song about

God I would sing for you, and I remember that I woke up singing this morning.

I pause the podcast as I try to remember and call back to my mind what I was singing when the sun shone through my eastern-facing bedroom window. I sang it for a while, just quietly to myself, as I made my bed and got going for the day. But what was it? I'm spinning through all the memories of my day, willing the lyrics to come back to me.

I knew I needed to remember. Because I knew, right there on the path, that I was supposed to go on this walk today, to hear this podcast, to remember the words I woke up singing, for God to give me the song for my next season. No wonder I couldn't get Radnor off my mind today, even with the stress-fractured foot and a bit of a glitch in my calendar which got me to the lake later than I usually go. The whispers of the Holy Spirit, pointing me toward that walk today, are clear to me now. But I'm dying to remember what the song was!

I start walking again, hoping my mind will bring it back to the front as I knew it was the Holy Spirit reminding me of the song this morning.

Oh yes!, I think as it finally comes to me. *I played the song when I got to the office this morning. "We Dance."* I still don't remember the exact lyrics, but I remember the song. It's a deep cut from the *You Make Me Brave* worship album. I finish the last ten minutes of the podcast sermon, and as I cross over the lake on the metal bridge, the podcast ends, and I scroll through my music to "We Dance."

Tears pour as I hear the lyrics I woke up singing that very morning...

And I will lock eyes with the One who's ransomed me,
the One who gave me joy for mourning.

And I will lock eyes with the One who's chosen me,
the One who set my feet to dancing.[10]

And don't you know that's exactly my story. That's 100 percent who I am today and where I am today.

He ransomed me. Jesus paid for me with His life so that I would belong to no one else. Even if the deal didn't come with the promise of eternity, which it does, I would take it and be deeply grateful because He has made my life worth living.

And I want, more than anything else, to lock eyes with this God who has taken my mourning and turned it into joy. When I persevered, when I hung on through the pain, when I willingly handed Him my hurts from over the years and the new ones birthed, He gave me joy, the difference in size like a watermelon seed of mourning to a massive colorful watermelon of joy.

And He set my feet to dancing. The girl who was too insecure to let loose on the dance floor, the one who felt too heavy to move with grace or ease, the one who has had to push through the hurt and the fear to a place of freedom? God set her feet, my feet, to dancing.

Maybe that's the moral of this whole thing. Maybe the most beautiful thing we can look at, in order to persevere, finish, thrive, live, is the eyes of our God. So if you need me, that's where I hope you always find me. Locking eyes with the One who has chosen me.

And so I leave you with that. We have looked for lovely and found it. We have resolved to be the kind of women that do not quit, that do not give up, that strengthen our minds and hearts to let the work God is doing in us come to completion.

This is my story.

This is my song.

Praising my Savior all the day long.

THANK YOU

I love writing this part of every book because I want you to know my people, and I want a place where I get to personally thank each of the humans that put up with me on a regular basis.

So I end this book with deepest gratitude and so much thanks:

To Justin Bieber and James Corden, for making my favorite video on the Internet, one that I managed to watch at some point every day of writing this book.

To Hillsong United for *Empires* and Bethel Music for *We Will Not Be Shaken*. Both albums shaped and molded me throughout 2015 and had massive impact on the cadence of these pages. Other musicians I'm deeply grateful to: Mumford & Sons, Dave Barnes, Ben Rector, Taylor Swift, Ryan Adams, Matt Wertz, Sam Hunt, Hillsong Young & Free, Andrew Ripp, Lady Antebellum, Amanda Cook, and the soundtrack to *Saving Mr. Banks* (which is AMAZING if you haven't heard it).

To the people at the Ryman Auditorium for allowing me to sit in section 15 for a few hours and then hop down to section 2, and write about my favorite place in this city.

To my counselor, Jennifer, for walking some treacherous roads with me and refusing to give up on my healing. You have truly been a godsend.

To Israel Collective and my bus buddies for making my first trip to Israel one of the most memorable experiences of my entire life. Summer camp feelings or not, I love your guts. Next year in Jerusalem.

To Lisa, Hillary, Jennifer, and Heather. Your editing voices and wise suggestions have transformed this book into what it was meant to be. And to all the wonderful humans at B&H and LifeWay, I feel so honored to be part of the family.

To the wonderful team of folks who keep my head above water, my calendar synced, and my heart in check—Leigh Holt and everyone at MaddJett, Lisa Jackson, Brian Elliott, Brian Smith, Kyle, Kelli, Keith, Sarah, Eliza, and April.

To my family and dear friends for all your love and support. From Denton to Edinburgh, from Athens to Nashville, from Marietta to New York, and all the stops in between. Without you I wouldn't want to write; I just wouldn't love my stories if you weren't in them.

To you, my reader friend, for always showing up. Your kindness to read this far matters more to me than you will ever know.

While writing this book, I spent significant time in New York City. One afternoon I walked by a spray-painted sign that read "NY never leaves you." That's true in my heart. When I'm looking for creative inspiration and when I'm looking for rest, I find them both there in generous measure. Thanks to New York for being where this book stirred up and poured out.

To Jesus. You saved me once, but You rescue me all the time. My flesh and my heart fail us both repeatedly, but You are the strength of my heart. You are my portion forever. I'm so glad to do this life with You. When I really looked for lovely, I found You.

NOTES

1. Annie F. Downs, *Let's All Be Brave* (Grand Rapids, MI: Zondervan, 2014).

2. For deeper study, see Psalm 139:13–14, Ephesians 2:10, and Isaiah 45:12.

3. See https://www.psychologytoday.com/blog/the-athletes-way/201312/why-do-the-songs-your-past-evoke-such-vivid-memories.

4. "Cares Chorus," from Psalty's Funtastic Praise Party, see http://www.psalty.com/track/689448/cares-chorus?feature_id=140960.

5. Author wrote a similar chapter titled "Mango-Colored Nail Polish" in *180: Stories of People Who Changed Their Lives by Changing Their Minds* (Kansas City, MO: The House Studio, 2010).

6. See http://giverny.org/monet/home.

7. See http://www.moma.org/visit/calendar/exhibitions/963.

8. See http://laplazacultural.com/#1.

9. Author also wrote a version of this for (in)Courage. See http://www.incourage.me/2014/09/trust-the-path.html.

10. "We Dance, " written by Steffany Gretzinger and Amanda Cook, 2013 Bethel Music Publishing, see https://bethelmusic.com/albums/you-make-me-brave.

If you loved this book,
GO DEEPER WITH THE BIBLE STUDY.

A 7-session study for women who long to live as if they fully believe in this truth: God makes everything beautiful in His time.

JOIN ANNIE F. DOWNS IN THIS STUDY IF YOU WANT TO:
- Discover the beauty in the mundane and difficult moments of life
- Develop a more personal relationship with God as you discover scriptural truths
- Grow spiritually through individual study time and group sessions
- Understand God sometimes calls us to do hard, but ultimately rewarding, tasks
- Learn to laugh through times of perseverance and see the beauty of the journey

For more information, visit **AnnieFDowns.com**